180

Devotional

Direction

Turn Your Eyes Upon Jesus

Alan James Schrader

180° DEVOTIONAL DIRECTION

Turn Your Eyes Upon Jesus

Second Edition: November 2021

Printed in the United States of America

ISBN:9798757154695

FORWARD

It is imperative to keep our eyes on Jesus, especially in the middle of a storm; It can be life or death to our souls. Peter and his friends were in a boat, and a storm came up suddenly. Some storms can be seen coming, while other storms happen with no warning.

No matter the kind of storm you find yourself in, search for Jesus. He is with you in your storm, but you must seek to see Him and then work not to lose sight of Him. Some storms are so loud and tumultuous that keeping our focus on Him is an actual workout. There is resistance and consistency involved.

Storms can come to us individually, to a whole community, statewide and nationally, and even worldwide. We must resist the temptation of storm watching. Measuring the height of the waves, the speed of the wind, the temperature of the water, and seeking to know the barometric pressure can be all-consuming. Yet, storm watching is what comes naturally because it is looming all around us. The truth is, all the details of what, who, where, when, why of our life storms will keep our mind and soul on the natural instead of the supernatural. And eventually, be detrimental to our faith. It doesn't take faith to storm watch or to state the obvious.

Searching for Jesus and making him our focus and pursuit in our storm puts our faith to work. We must consistently be looking to Jesus, who will keep our souls from being overwhelmed and full of fear and dismay (Keeping our eyes on Jesus, the author, and finisher of our faith). Just as you are tempted to focus on all the details of your storm, focus on the character of Jesus. Who has He said He is in His word?

4

Search that out. What has He promised to do for those who put their hope and faith in Him? Keep searching, and He will be found! And, herein is found rest for your soul. Consistently searching and finding Him to be all He promised and that He fulfills every promise He has made in His word is the only way through the storm.

I believe Chaplain Alan's devotional book will be a tool that will help you to keep your focus. The Word of God is brought forth on every page. I pray that it would be a blessing to you as it has been to me.

Love,
Mary J. Schrader
(Wife of the Chaplain)

DAY 1

The Lord Working With Them

"And they went out and preached everywhere, the Lord working with them and confirming the word through the accompanying signs. Amen." Mark 16:20

Did you love your last job? For many, the answer is, unfortunately, NO! The truth is, it would be sad to go to work daily in drudgery. Even worse would be working with people that hate their job too. However, for the believer, when we realize who we work for and who is working with us, we love going to work.

Reread these beautiful words: The Lord working with them and confirm the word through the accompanying signs: The disciples did what Jesus told them to do, and Jesus then did what only He could do – the accompanying signs. So when we go out to do the work of God, Jesus will work with us. They went out and preached everywhere: This means that they didn't remain together to bless each other; they went out. The followers of Jesus should come together, but they come together to properly equip them to go out and touch a needy world.

My prayer for us today is that we take comfort knowing this: "teaching them to observe all things that I have commanded you; and lo, I am with you always, even to the end of the age." Amen." Matthew 28:2

DAY 2

God Be Thanked

"But God be thanked that though you were slaves of sin, yet you obeyed from the heart that form of doctrine to which you were delivered. And having been set free from sin, you became slaves of righteousness." Romans 6:17-18

Notice how Paul puts it in the past tense (you were slaves) because we have been freed from slavery to sin. He also says that we have been set free by faith, which he describes as obedience from the heart. The trust is placed in God's Word, which he describes as that form of doctrine. All in all, the point is clear: You put your faith in God's Word and walk in His Spirit, and now you are set free. "For what the law could not do in that it was weak through the flesh, God did by sending His own Son in the likeness of sinful flesh, on account of sin: He condemned sin in the flesh, that the righteous requirement of the law might be fulfilled in us who do not walk according to the flesh but according to the Spirit." Romans 8:3-4

We need to understand this because Jesus fulfilled the righteous requirement of the law, and because we are in Christ, we fulfill the law by faith. The law is fulfilled in us concerning obedience because Jesus' righteousness stands for ours. The law is fulfilled in us regarding punishment because any punishment demanded by the law was poured out upon Jesus. Paul does not say that we fulfill the righteous requirement of the law. Instead, he carefully states that the righteous requirement of the law is fulfilled in us. It isn't fulfilled by us but in us.

Simply put, Jesus is our substitute. Jesus was treated as a sinner so we could be treated as righteous. Notice, Paul says, "In us who do not walk according to the flesh but according to the Spirit." Their life is marked by obedience to the Holy Spirit, not by adherence to the flesh. In other words, people who enjoy freedom do not walk according to the flesh but according to the Spirit.

My prayer of thanks today is: "But thanks be to God, who gives us the victory through our Lord Jesus Christ." 1 Corinthians 15:57

DAY 3

Love, More Than A Feeling

"And this I pray, that your love may abound still more and more in knowledge and all discernment, that you may approve the things that are excellent, that you may be sincere and without offense till the day of Christ," Philippians 1:9-10

Notice how the love that Paul desired to abound in the Philippians was not "blind love." Instead, it was love that knew the divine. In other words, it could discern beyond the senses and the intellect. This love that abounds in knowledge and discernment has everything to do with knowing who God is and what HE has done.

"Beloved, let us love one another, for love is of God; and everyone who loves is born of God and knows God. He who does not love does not know God, for God is love. In this, the love of God was manifested toward us, that God has sent His only begotten Son into the world, that we might live through Him. In this is love, not that we loved God, but that He loved us and sent His Son to be the propitiation for our sins. Beloved, if God so loved us, we also ought to love one another. 1 John 4:7-11

Today, I pray that we love one another because we are loved by God and have received that love and live in light of it.

DAY 4

The Accursed Things

"But the children of Israel committed a trespass regarding the accursed things, for Achan the son of Carmi, the son of Zabdi, the son of Zerah, of the tribe of Judah, took of the accursed things; so the anger of the LORD burned against the children of Israel." Joshua 7:1

It is painful to think about your sin being the cause of others not receiving victory. Unfortunately, this story reminds us of this sad truth. For example, Joshua commanded the nation in Joshua 6:18 that they should not take any of the accursed things. Israel's success depended on their willingness to obey and keep the instructions of the LORD; Achan's rebellion and unwillingness to following God fully - caused the people to experience defeat. For example, the thirty-six men killed (7:5) were thirty-six more than were killed at Jericho, which many viewed as a much more difficult city to conquer. Though this number was small from a military standpoint, it was devastating to Israel. Moreover, it meant that Israel could be defeated in the Promised Land.

The defeat at Ai showed that what mattered was not the opponent's strength but the help of the LORD. Without God's help, the people were vulnerable to defeat.

"Get up, sanctify the people, and say, 'Sanctify yourselves for tomorrow, because thus says the LORD God of Israel: 'There is an accursed thing in your midst, O Israel; you cannot stand before your enemies until you take away the accursed thing from among you.'" Joshua 7:13

My prayer for us today is that we remember the command given through Joshua: "And you, by all means, abstain from the accursed things, lest you become accursed when you take of the accursed things, and make the camp of Israel a curse, and trouble it." Joshua 6:18

DAY 5

All Nations

"After these things I looked, and behold, a great multitude which no one could number, of all nations, tribes, peoples, and tongues, standing before the throne and before the Lamb, clothed with white robes, with palm branches in their hands, and crying out with a loud voice, saying, "Salvation belongs to our God who sits on the throne, and to the Lamb!"
Revelation 7:9-10

I love reading this: "A great multitude which no one could number, of all nations, tribes, peoples, and tongues." What a beautiful gathering this will be. The diversity here is evidence that the Great Commission will be fulfilled before the end, even as Jesus promised: "And this gospel of the kingdom will be preached in all the world as a witness to all the nations, and then the end will come" (Matthew 24:14). Because John knew they came from different nations, tribes, peoples, and tongues, we know that there will be differences among people in heaven, just as there is on earth. We will not all be the same. God's plan is inspiring to me.

Notice also the Palm branches in their hands. These should remind us of Jesus' triumphal entry into Jerusalem (John 12:12-16), where the people cried out Hosanna, and Jesus is praised as Savior and King. The word Hosanna means "save now!" Palm branches were emblems of victory. It shows that this great multitude celebrated a great triumph as Jesus came into Jerusalem.

This truth is the hope of ALL NATIONS: "The city had no need of the sun or of the moon to shine in it, for the glory of God illuminated it. The Lamb is its light. And the nations of those who are saved shall walk in its light, and the kings of the earth bring their glory and honor into it. Its gates shall not be shut at all by day (there shall be no night there). And they shall bring the glory and the honor of the nations into it. But there shall by no means enter it anything that defiles or causes an abomination or a lie, but only those who are written in the Lamb's Book of Life." Revelation 21:23-27

My prayer for us today is that we would have a love for ALL Nations.

DAY 6

Guard From Deception

"Now as He sat on the Mount of Olives, the disciples came to Him privately, saying, "Tell us, when will these things be? And what will be the sign of Your coming, and of the end of the age?" And Jesus answered and said to them: "Take heed that no one deceives you. For many will come in My name, saying, 'I am the Christ,' and will deceive many." Matthew 24:3-5

Notice how when the disciples asked Jesus about the last days, he mentioned deception. The Greek word for deceives in this verse is planao. According to Strong's concordance, it means "to (properly, cause to) roam (from safety, truth, or virtue): - go astray, deceive, err, seduce, wander, be out of the way."

From the outset, Jesus warned the disciples that many people would be deceived as they anticipated His return. But, unfortunately, there have been times in the church's history when rash predictions were made and then relied upon, resulting in great disappointment, disillusionment, and falling way. The truth is, these predictors ultimately took people away from doing God's Word and caused them to trust in man's knowledge and charisma.

In the Gospels, Jesus makes the following warnings:

"Watch therefore, for you know neither the day nor the hour in which the Son of Man is coming." Matthew 25:13

14

"Therefore you also be ready, for the Son of Man is coming at an hour you do not expect....Blessed is that servant whom his master will find so doing when he comes." Luke 12:40, 43

Besides praying, what are we to be "doing"? "Then the King will say to those on His right hand, 'Come, you blessed of My Father, inherit the kingdom prepared for you from the foundation of the world: for I was hungry and you gave Me food; I was thirsty and you gave Me drink; I was a stranger and you took Me in; I was naked and you clothed Me; I was sick and you visited Me; I was in prison and you came to Me.'....And the King will answer and say to them, 'Assuredly, I say to you, inasmuch as you did it to one of the least of these My brethren, you did it to Me.'" Matthew 25:34-40

✱ Today, I pray that we would NOT be kept from doing what God has called us to do.

DAY 7

Beauty

"One thing I have desired of the LORD, That will I seek: That I may dwell in the house of the LORD All the days of my life, To behold the beauty of the LORD, And to inquire in His temple." Psalm 27:4

The things we desire and seek after can make us or break us. The truth is, where and in whom we find beauty is significant to the health of our soul.

David was known as a man after God's own heart (see 1 Samual 13:14 & Acts 13:22). I believe one of the reasons for this characteristic is that David knew something of the beauty of the Lord, the eternal and supreme pleasantness of the divine being and perfections: His holiness is his beauty ("Your people shall be volunteers In the day of Your power; In the beauties of holiness, from the womb of the morning, You have the dew of Your youth." Psalm 110:3); His goodness is His beauty ("For how great is its goodness And how great its beauty! Grain shall make the young men thrive, And new wine the young women." Zechariah 9:17).

David's prayer for this "one desire" brought him into a beauty that cannot be compared with any other.

My prayer for us today is that we: "Give unto the LORD the glory due to His name; Worship the LORD in the beauty of holiness." Psalm 29:2

DAY 8

Give Them Something

"When it was evening, His disciples came to Him, saying, 'This is a deserted place, and the hour is already late. Send the multitudes away, that they may go into the villages and buy themselves food.' But Jesus said to them, 'They do not need to go away. You give them something to eat.'" Matthew 14:15-16

When the disciples see the massive crowd of people present as the mealtime approached, they ask Jesus to send everyone away to a nearby village to buy food. However, Jesus responds with, "They need not go away; you give them something to eat." They'd heard Him teaching about faith numerous times, and now it seems He wants to ignite theirs by reaffirming His promises. So they collect five loaves and two fish. Jesus blessed the meal and multiplied it to feed everyone present. And to make the point clear, there are twelve baskets left over, one for each of them. The prominence of this story, which is recorded in all four gospels, shows that both the Holy Spirit and the early church thought this story was important.

Two things stand out to me about this story today:
1 - It shows that Jesus had compassion and care for the people of God and wanted them to know His provision in their lives.
2 - It shows that Jesus chose to work through the disciples' hands to testify of God's provision and care.

My prayer for us today is that we would boast in God's compassion and provision.

DAY 9

In Heaven

"In this manner, therefore, pray: Our Father in heaven, Hallowed be Your name." Matthew 6:9

First, we have to know that Heaven is real. It's where God lives. When Jesus said, "Our Father in heaven," He was connecting us to where our Father is. He lifts our focus to the throne room in Heaven. Jesus is in Heaven, sitting at God's right hand. Heaven is where God rules, where He sits enthroned. It's a place of dominion, authority, and power over every principality and stronghold. Here is why the Apostle Paul admonishes the Colossians with this: "If then you were raised with Christ, seek those things which are above, where Christ is, sitting at the right hand of God. Set your mind on things above, not on things on the earth." Colossians 3:1-2

The best example for Christian living comes from minds that are fixed on Heaven. A mind set on Heaven realizes that their lives are hidden with Christ in God. Given that Jesus is enthroned in Heaven, their thoughts and hearts are now connected to Jesus. Jesus looked forward to Heaven, and so should we – recognizing that our citizenship is in Heaven. I know this to be true because He said these words: "In My Father's house are many mansions; if it were not so, I would have told you. I go to prepare a place for you. And if I go and prepare a place for you, I will come again and receive you to Myself; that where I am, there you may be also." John 14:2-3

My prayer for us today is that we set our minds on things that are above.

DAY 10

You Were Called

"I, therefore, the prisoner of the Lord, beseech you to walk worthy of the calling with which you were called, with all lowliness and gentleness, with longsuffering, bearing with one another in love, endeavoring to keep the unity of the Spirit in the bond of peace." Ephesians 4:1-3

Have you ever paused to consider your calling, where Jesus has uniquely appointed you to serve on behalf of Himself and His Kingdom within society? Another way to ask the question is, how does Jesus express Himself through you as His ambassador to the world around you?

In our daily walk, does how we relate and serve people reflect the ways of Jesus? To answer this question, you must know who Jesus is personally. Then, you and I have the great privilege of showing His love, joy, peace, patience, kindness, goodness, faithfulness, gentleness, self-control through our calling. A worthy walk before God will be marked by lowliness and gentleness, not a pushy desire to defend our rights and advance our agenda. This humble, forgiving attitude towards each other naturally fulfills this gift of the unity of the Spirit.

My prayer for us today is that we understand our calling and all that Christ did to empower us to walk in it.

DAY 11

Divine Delay

"Beloved, I now write to you this second epistle (in both of which I stir up your pure minds by way of reminder), that you may be mindful of the words which were spoken before by the holy prophets, and of the commandment of us, the apostles of the Lord and Savior, knowing this first: that scoffers will come in the last days, walking according to their own lusts, and saying, 'Where is the promise of His coming? For since the fathers fell asleep, all things continue as they were from the beginning of creation.'" 2 Peter 3:1-4

The Apostle Peter wrote his second letter to a church under persecution by an evil empire whose leaders descended into great darkness, demanded worship, and persecuted the Church. Peter began with a reminder that the words spoken by the biblical prophets are all true and will come to pass. Though these words are accurate, mockers will arrive who ridicule with their words because of a "divine delay." There is a temptation to believe that what God has spoken is inaccurate because of the delay, but the "delay" has a divine purpose. "The Lord is not slack concerning His promise, as some count slackness, but is long-suffering toward us, not willing that any should perish but that all should come to repentance. But the day of the Lord will come as a thief in the night, in which the heavens will pass away with a great noise, and the elements will melt with fervent heat; both the earth and the works that are in it will be burned up." 2 Peter 3:9-10

The same word of God that created all matter and judged the world in the Great Flood will one day bring a judgment of fire upon the earth. The truth is, God will keep His promise, and without delay, but according to His timing. The wait is due to the long-suffering of God, who allows man as much time as possible to repent.

My prayer is that we would see that the reason why Jesus' return isn't sooner is that all should come to repentance because God is not willing that any should perish.

DAY 12

Understand It Clearly

"The anger of the LORD will not turn back Until He has executed and performed the thoughts of His heart. In the latter days you will understand it perfectly." Jeremiah 23:20

What are we to understand perfectly? What are the thoughts of God's heart regarding His "fierce anger"? "The fierce anger of the LORD will not return until He has done it, And until He has performed the intents of His heart. In the latter days, you will consider it." Jeremiah 30:24

God's message to Jeremiah was clear: He wants us to understand His judgments so we can know His ways and cooperate with Him. Jeremiah had to prophesy judgment, but he was also commanded to intercede for God's fulfillment of His promises. In other words, the same Lord who would bring their judgment would bring their salvation. The truth is, the dispersion of Israel resulted from God's judgments in Jeremiah's day. However, His judgments set the stage for HIS salvation. The message is also evident today. God's judgments will come and have their full effect, but He will save a remnant during His judgments.

My prayer for us today is that we look to understand clearly God's promises: "But I will gather the remnant of My flock out of all countries where I have driven them, and bring them back to their folds; and they shall be fruitful and increase. I will set up shepherds over them who will feed them; and they shall fear no more, nor be dismayed, nor shall they be lacking," says the LORD." Jeremiah 23:3-4

DAY 13

Thieves & Robbers

"All who ever came before Me are thieves and robbers, but the sheep did not hear them. I am the door. If anyone enters by Me, he will be saved, and will go in and out and find pasture. The thief does not come except to steal, and to kill, and to destroy. I have come that they may have life, and that they may have it more abundantly." John 10:8-10

Have you ever had something stolen from you? Almost 50 years later, I still remember when someone stole my new orange bike from my yard. I was only a little kid, but this terrible experience impacted that it is Etched in my memory. Thieves and robbers do such damage to our souls if we let them.

The Apostle John records Jesus saying, "All who ever came before Me are thieves and robbers." Thief implies deception and trickery; robber implies violence and destruction.

Jesus explained that not everyone is a true shepherd; some are like thieves and robbers. One mark of their being a thief and a robber is how they gain entry among the sheep. The true shepherd comes in the legitimate and designed way: through love, calling, care, and sacrificial service.

I have come that they may have life, and they may have it more abundantly: Jesus said this to contrast His shepherd-like care with unfaithful and illegitimate leaders. They come to steal, and to kill, and to destroy. Jesus comes to bring life to

26

His people. Abundant life is a life of satisfaction and contentment in Jesus.

The life of the Great and Good Shepherd is always giving. It is for us he lives, and because he lives, we live also. He lives to plead for us. He lives to represent us in heaven. He lives to rule and reign in the Everlasting Kingdom that He invites us to be a part of today and throughout eternity.

My prayer is that we receive HIS pastoral care. "For you were like sheep going astray, but have now returned to the Shepherd and Overseer of your souls." 1 Peter 2:25

DAY 14

The Works of God

"Now as Jesus passed by, He saw a man who was blind from birth. And His disciples asked Him, saying, "Rabbi, who sinned, this man or his parents, that he was born blind?" Jesus answered, "Neither this man nor his parents sinned, but that the works of God should be revealed in him." John 9:1-3

A common belief in John's day was that calamity or suffering resulted from some great sin. Jesus, however, used this man's suffering to teach about the "works of God." Christ heals the blind man to build faith and reveal the Glory of God.

In John 9, we see four different reactions to the "works of God" demonstrated.
1. The neighbors (v.8) are surprised and apprehensive.
2. The Pharisees showed unbelief and hardness of heart.
3. The parents believed but kept quiet for fear of ex-communication from the synagogue.
4. The healed man showed teachableness and growing faith.

The man healed of blindness had his faith tested by the religious leaders. He was cursed and thrown out of the synagogue. This experience should remind all of us that persecution may come when we follow Jesus Christ. We may lose friends; we may even lose our lives. But no one can ever take away the gift of eternal life found in receiving Jesus Christ.

My prayer for us today is that we would give thanks for the beautiful works of God. "Oh, that men would give thanks to the LORD for His goodness, And for His wonderful works to the children of men!" Psalm 107:8

DAY 15

Thank You For Making Me

"You made all the delicate, inner parts of my body and knit me together in my mother's womb. Thank you for making me so wonderfully complex! Your workmanship is in marvelous— how well I know it. You watched me as I was being formed in utter seclusion, as I was woven together in the dark of the womb. You saw me before I was born. Every day of my life was recorded in your book. Every moment was laid out before a single day had passed. How precious are your thoughts about me, O God. They cannot be numbered! I can't even count them; they outnumber the grains of sand! And when I wake up, you are still with me!" Psalm 139:13-18 NLT

The Psalmist is declaring that God made us, and therefore He knows all about us. So let's review some questions and answers from the scriptures:

How are we made?
"This is the book of the genealogy of Adam. In the day that God created man, He made him in the likeness of God." Genesis 5:1

To whom are we made?
"The earth is the LORD's, and all its fullness, The world and those who dwell therein." Psalm 24:1

What is the Problem?

"Therefore, just as through one man sin entered the world, and death through sin, and thus death spread to all men because all sinned—" Romans 5:12

What is God's Plan?

"For God so loved the world that He gave His only begotten Son, that whoever believes in Him should not perish but have everlasting life." John 3:16

"For whoever calls on the name of the LORD shall be saved." Romans 10:13

My prayer for us today is that we find the answers to life from GOD'S WORD.

DAY 16

Written In The Books

"And I saw the dead, small and great, standing before God, and books were opened. And another book was opened, which is the Book of Life. And the dead were judged according to their works, by the things which were written in the books." Revelation 20:12

I've heard many people through the years say, "I should write a book." Well, a book is being written about our lives. Our story is being recorded, and the One who is writing things down is very accurate.

It should be evident for each one of us that Christ will judge the secrets of all men according to what is written of our lives. Remember, Hebrews 9:27 says, "it is appointed for men to die once but after this the judgment."

Also, it is clearly stated: "And whosoever was not found written in the book of life was cast into the lake of fire." Revelation 20:15

In the book of Luke, we read how the disciples reported to Jesus their great excitement because the devils were subject to them in His name. However, Jesus told His disciples this: "Don't rejoice that the spirits are subject unto you; but rather rejoice, because your names are written in heaven." Luke 10:20

One thing that you want to be sure of is that your name is written in the book of life when your time comes to leave this earth or when Jesus comes for His church.

My prayer for us today is that we receive HIS Word: "For God so loved the world that He gave His only begotten Son, that whoever believes in Him should not perish but have everlasting life." "And this is eternal life, that they may know You, the only true God, and Jesus Christ whom You have sent." John 3:16; John 17:3

DAY 17

Nothing Wasted In God

"And being in Bethany at the house of Simon the leper, as He sat at the table, a woman came having an alabaster flask of very costly oil of spikenard. Then she broke the flask and poured it on His head. But there were some who were indignant among themselves, and said, 'Why was this fragrant oil wasted? For it might have been sold for more than three hundred denarii and given to the poor.' And they criticized her sharply." Mark 14:3-5

Having an alabaster flask of very costly oil: This was an extravagant display of devotion to Jesus. Often spices and ointments were used as investments. This particular alabaster flask seems to have been worth more than a year's wages for a laborer.

Some were indignant: It is believed that Judas may have started this criticism, but he wasn't alone for long. Mark, in his gospel, made it clear that they criticized her sharply. Each one looked at the oil on Jesus' head and considered it wasted.

Interestingly, the word translated 'waste' in Mark 14:4 is translated 'perdition' in John 17:12 and applied to Judas! So Judas criticized Mary for 'wasting money,' but then he went out and wasted his entire life!

Let her alone. Why do you trouble her? She has done a good work for Me: The disciples thought that this extravagant anointing with oil was a waste, but Jesus received it as good

34

work. With her simple love and devotion to Jesus, Mary understood what the disciples did not – that Jesus was about to die, and she intended this gift as a preparation for his burial.

Today, I pray that we know that what we do for Christ will never be wasted, no matter how others may criticize. "Watch, stand fast in the faith, be brave, be strong. Let all that you do be done with love." 1 Corinthians 16:13-14

DAY 18

His Reward

"Take heed that you do not do your charitable deeds before men, to be seen by them. Otherwise you have no reward from your Father in heaven. Therefore, when you do a charitable deed, do not sound a trumpet before you as the hypocrites do in the synagogues and in the streets, that they may have glory from men. Assuredly, I say to you, they have their reward. But when you do a charitable deed, do not let your left hand know what your right hand is doing, that your charitable deed may be in secret; and your Father who sees in secret will Himself reward you openly." Matthew 6:1-4

What reward do you desire? Who do you live to please? These are questions that we should ask so that our life's journey is not lived in vain.

In this passage, Charitable deeds can also be translated as righteousness. Jesus tells us not to do righteous things for the sake of display or image (to be seen by them). This admonition does not contradict His previous command to let your light shine before men (Matthew 5:16). Although Followers of Christ are too good works, they must not do good works only to be seen by men. Otherwise, you have no reward from your Father in heaven: The idea is when we do righteous deeds for the attention and applause of men, their attention and applause is our reward. It is much better to receive a prize from your Father in heaven. "And your Father who sees in secret will Himself reward you openly." It is HIS reward that we should desire and pursue.

36

The bottom line is that God cares about how we do our good works and, even more importantly, the motive we do them.

My prayer for us today is that we desire HIS rewards: "For the Son of Man will come in the glory of His Father with His angels, and then He will reward each according to his works." Matthew 16:27

DAY 19

Love Does No Harm To A Neighbor

"Owe no one anything except to love one another, for he who loves another has fulfilled the law. For the commandments, 'You shall not commit adultery,' 'You shall not murder,' 'You shall not steal,' 'You shall not bear false witness,' 'You shall not covet,' and if there is any other commandment, are all summed up in this saying, namely, 'You shall love your neighbor as yourself.' Love does no harm to a neighbor; therefore love is the fulfillment of the law.'" Romans 13:8-10

Those of us who are on social media, radio, or watch the news are well aware of the demeaning rhetoric that continues to go on. Calling each other derogatory names, cursing one another, and deliberately trying to devalue one another is the opposite of the Christians call.

The Bible reminds us: "Do not speak evil of one another, brethren. He who speaks evil of a brother and judges his brother speaks evil of the law and judges the law. But if you judge the law, you are not a doer of the law but a judge." James 4:11

We need to guard our hearts and minds against the devil's tactics and schemes to get us caught up in social gossip that will poison our souls. "Be sober, be vigilant; because your adversary the devil walks about like a roaring lion, seeking whom he may devour." 1 Peter 5:8

The devil would love to fill our hearts with hate. Remember, he is the father of lies, the one who feeds confusion and who sows discord. Don't allow his tactics to become yours. "Put on the whole armor of God, that you may be able to stand against the wiles of the devil." Ephesians 6:11

My prayer for us today is that we would: "Be anxious for nothing, but in everything by prayer and supplication, with thanksgiving, let your requests be made known to God; and the peace of God, which surpasses all understanding, will guard your hearts and minds through Christ Jesus." Philippians 4:6-7

DAY 20

Things That God Hates, Why?

"These six things the LORD hates, Yes, seven are an abomination to Him: A proud look, A lying tongue, Hands that shed innocent blood, A heart that devises wicked plans, Feet that are swift in running to evil, A false witness who speaks lies, And one who sows discord among brethren." Proverbs 6:16-19

The seven abominations are a severe list of things God hates. Have you ever asked the question, why? Another scripture comes to mind: "'For the LORD God of Israel says that He hates divorce, For it covers one's garment with violence,' Says the LORD of hosts. 'Therefore take heed to your spirit, That you do not deal treacherously.'" Malachi 2:16

Again, we read of something that God hates. Why? Could it be because the very things that God created are being destroyed today? Think about it, what is destroyed when the man is involved in the things God hates? Here is my list: RELATIONSHIP, FELLOWSHIP, FRIENDSHIP, PARTNERSHIP. These are some of the reasons we were created—no wonder the devil's temptation and deception are so strong in these areas. "The thief does not come except to steal, and to kill, and to destroy. I have come that they may have life and that they may have it more abundantly." John 10:10

My prayer: "Therefore put to death your members which are on the earth: fornication, uncleanness, passion, evil desire, and covetousness, which is idolatry. Because of these things the wrath of God is coming upon the sons of disobedience, in which you yourselves once walked when you lived in them. But now you yourselves are to put off all these: anger, wrath, malice, blasphemy, filthy language out of your mouth. Do not lie to one another, since you have put off the old man with his deeds, and have put on the new man who is renewed in knowledge according to the image of Him who created him," Colossians 3:5-10

DAY 21

HE Makes All Things New

"Then I, John, saw the holy city, New Jerusalem, coming down out of heaven from God, prepared as a bride adorned for her husband. And I heard a loud voice from heaven saying, 'Behold, the tabernacle of God is with men, and He will dwell with them, and they shall be His people. God Himself will be with them and be their God. And God will wipe away every tear from their eyes; there shall be no more death, nor sorrow, nor crying. There shall be no more pain, for the former things have passed away.' Then He who sat on the throne said, 'Behold, I make all things new.' And He said to me, 'Write, for these words are true and faithful.'"
Revelation 21:2-5

The first thing that I notice is that God is speaking directly from HIS THRONE. I believe HE is giving us a picture of HIS eternal plan. Behold, I make all things new: This statement is in the present tense, "I am making everything new."– to allow sin and its destruction to do a more significant work of making all things new. At this point (in the book of Revelation), His plan is complete. All things are new.

The Apostle Paul saw this transformation at work on this side of eternity: Therefore, we do not lose heart. Even though our outward man is perishing, yet the inward man is being renewed day by day... Therefore, if anyone is in Christ, he is a new creation; old things have passed away; behold, all things have become new (2 Corinthians 4:16, 5:17).

42

The last words that we need to take note of are: "these words are true and faithful." The voice from heaven wants John to "write" this down because it is sure. In other words, it is as if it were done already. In other words, we should take God's promise as present payment, and if HE has said from HIS throne that HE makes all things new, it is done.

My prayer for us today is that we BEHOLD what is TRUE and FAITHFUL - HE MAKES ALL THINGS NEW.

DAY 22

Windows in Heaven

"So an officer on whose hand the king leaned answered the man of God and said, "Look, if the LORD would make windows in heaven, could this thing be?" And he said, "In fact, you shall see it with your eyes, but you shall not eat of it." 2 Kings 7:2

Windows speak of transparency and openness. We use windows to see through and, in some cases, enter through. Windows can also speak of receiving blessings. The reference to the windows of heaven in the passage above reminded us of the glorious account of the provision in 2 Kings 7 when God provided in a completely unexpected way. "Look, if the Lord would make windows in heaven, could this thing be?" The king's officer, however, doubted the prophecy because his heart was filled with Unbelief:

All in all, the officer well illustrates the conduct of Unbelief:

· Unbelief dares to question the truthfulness of God's promise itself.
· Unbelief says, "This is a new thing and cannot be true."
· Unbelief says, "This is a sudden thing and cannot be true."
· Unbelief says, "There is no way to accomplish this thing."
· Unbelief says, "There is only one way God can work."

· Unbelief says, "Even if God does something, it won't be enough."

This story should speak to us that God has resources that we know nothing about, and it is often of no help to try and figure out - or worry about - how God will provide.

My prayer for us today is that we guard our hearts against Unbelief so that we experience blessings from the windows of heaven. "And try Me now in this, Says the LORD of hosts, If I will not open for you the windows of heaven And pour out for you such blessing That there will not be room enough to receive it." Malachi 3:10

DAY 23

Endure To Enter The Promises

*"For I know the thoughts that I think toward you, says the LORD, **thoughts of peace** and not of evil, to give you **a future** and **a hope**. Then you will call upon Me and go and pray to Me, and I will listen to you. And you will seek Me and find Me, when you search for Me with all your heart." Jeremiah 29:11-13*

We all enjoy the promises of having peace, hope, and a future. However, we have to endure to enter those promises through tests and temptations that can make or break us. In the book of Jeremiah, we learn that the people of God were in Babylon by the will of God, and He was bringing judgment on Judah for their generations of rebellion against Him (see Jeremiah 29:4-10). In God's plan, they would be in Babylon a long time, so it was best for them to settle in and make the best of their lives and families there. God wanted them to do good in their communities and be a blessing to their Babylonian neighbors.

I am convinced that what we learn before we enter into the fulfillment of His promises is critical. Embracing the trials, testings, and disciplines of God will cause us to grow in character and integrity. God had a particular purpose in allowing the captivity of his people into Babylon. The bottom line, God will not hide from His people when they seek Him. Most importantly, His people are called to know and experience HIS peace and hope, leading to a future.

My prayer for us today is: "...we also glory in tribulations, knowing that tribulation produces perseverance; and perseverance, character; and character, hope. Now hope does not disappoint because the love of God has been poured out in our hearts by the Holy Spirit who was given to us." Romans 5:3-5

DAY 24

The Grace Of Our Lord Jesus Christ
Be With You

"He who testifies to these things says, "Surely I am coming quickly." Amen. Even so, come, Lord Jesus! The grace of our Lord Jesus Christ be with you all. Amen." Revelation 22:20-21

This scripture may be the last recorded prayer in the Bible. Many scholars believe that the book of Revelation was one of the last recorded books of the New Testament period. Whether this is true or not, the concluding prayer is worth contemplating.

The book closes with John's longing for the return of Jesus for His people. If the statement "I am coming quickly" were not enough, Jesus emphasizes both sides – surely before and Amen after. However, the book ends with a prayer for the grace of the Lord Jesus Christ and His grace for all. Could it be that John is recognizing and reminding us of the need for grace in the hour before the return of Christ?

My prayer for us today is that we say Amen for the grace of our Lord Jesus Christ. "Let us therefore come boldly to the throne of grace, that we may obtain mercy and find grace to help in time of need." Hebrews 4:16

DAY 25

The Eye Of The LORD

"Behold, the eye of the LORD is on those who fear Him, On those who hope in His mercy," Psalm 33:18

The "eye of the LORD" has been defined as the observation of God. This passage further describes it as God's favor and delight on those who fear Him and those who hope in His mercy.

I used to sing an old song called "His Eye I On The Sparrow." The song comes from the principle in Matthew 10:29-30, "Are not two sparrows sold for a copper coin? And not one of them falls to the ground apart from your Father's will. But the very hairs of your head are all numbered. Do not fear therefore; you are of more value than many sparrows."

Jesus reminds His disciples that they didn't need to be afraid because He cared for them, even down to the most minute detail. If God's eye is on the sparrow and numbers the very hairs of our head, then He will also pay careful attention to those who hope in Him. So we read in Psalm 147:11, "The LORD takes pleasure in those who fear Him, In those who hope in His mercy."

My prayer for us today is that we would be hopeful in knowing that His eye is upon us.

DAY 26

Trust In You

"But let all those rejoice who put their trust in You; Let them ever shout for joy, because You defend them; Let those also who love Your name Be joyful in You. For You, O LORD, will bless the righteous; With favor You will surround him as with a shield." Psalm 5:11-12

Who and what we place our trust in is very significant to the health and well-being of our soul. Trust is defined this way in Strong's: to flee for protection; figuratively, to confide in:— have hope, take refuge, (put) trust.

The Psalmist reminds us that the righteous are those who place their trust in the LORD and love His name. Their righteousness is evident in their words. They rejoice, they shout for joy, and they are joyful in the LORD. The truth is the measure that we maintain our joy will be strong in the Lord and for the Lord.

The Psalmist reminds us, "You, O Lord, will bless the righteous; with favor, You will surround him." Knowing that God looks on us with favor and pleasure is the greatest blessing and knowledge we can receive. This favor is our standing in grace. It is in this hope we place our trust.

My prayer for us today is: "Trust in the LORD with all your heart, And lean not on your own understanding; In all your ways acknowledge Him, And He shall direct your paths. Do not be wise in your own eyes; Fear the LORD and depart from evil." Proverbs 3:5-7

DAY 27

You Have Put Gladness In My Heart

*"There are many who say, "Who will show us any good?"
LORD, lift up the light of Your countenance upon us. You
have put gladness in my heart, More than in the season that
their grain and wine increased. I will both lie down in peace,
and sleep; For You alone, O LORD, make me dwell in
safety." Psalm 4:6-8*

I love how the Psalms can capture the heart of man. After the
continual disappointment from the world, one can begin to
doubt if God will show us any good. However, despite what
man says or the world does, we can trust that the LORD will
deliver on His goodness. So David, the Psalmist, prays:
"LORD, lift up the light of Your countenance upon us."

I believe David is praying and proclaiming the Aaronic
promise of blessing found in Numbers 6:24-26: "The LORD
bless you and keep you; The LORD make His face shine
upon you, And be gracious to you; The LORD lift up His
countenance upon you, And give you peace." When we know
that the face of God shines favorably on us, it puts gladness in
our hearts. So though David was in distress, oppressed by
ungodly men all around, he could still have delight in his
heart because the LORD was shining upon him and giving
him peace. So when HIS gladness is in our hearts, we dwell
in safety.

My prayer for us today is: "God be merciful to us and bless
us, And cause His face to shine upon us, Selah" Psalm 67:1

52

DAY 28

You, O LORD, Are A Shield For Me

"LORD, how they have increased who trouble me! Many are they who rise up against me. Many are they who say of me, " There is no help for him in God." Selah But You, O LORD, are a shield for me, My glory and the One who lifts up my head. I cried to the LORD with my voice, And He heard me from His holy hill. Selah" Psalm 3:1-4

Have you ever felt unprotected and surrounded by an enemy? At the writing of this Psalm, David was experiencing this type of trouble. His son led what seemed to be a successful rebellion against him. We also learn that many of his previous friends and associates also turned on him. They joined the party of those who troubled him (2 Samuel 15:13). David's situation was so bad that others were saying that he was beyond God's help. Those who said this probably didn't feel that God could help. Why does a teacher ask a question that they already have the answer to the question? Yes, it's for the student to gain perspective and knowledge that will help transform their thinking.

The Psalmist seems genuinely mystified in asking the question. The questioner knows that the nations have no reason to rage against God, and they have no benefit in raging against Him. They oppose both the LORD and His Anointed. Anointed speaks of Christ, the Anointed One. Since Jesus is the perfect representation of the Father (John 10:30, 14:9) if you oppose God the Father, you oppose Jesus. If you oppose

Jesus, you oppose God the Father. Therefore, their opposition against God is nothing but a vain thing.

The response to the question is that God laughs because He sits in the heavens. It isn't just an earthly throne He occupies; it is the throne of heaven with authority over all creation. In other words, what does heaven have to fear from earth?

The sad truth is that many have opposed God and His Kingdom in Jesus Christ through the centuries. However, each one of these opponents has been frustrated and crushed. Why? Because "The LORD shall hold them in derision."

My prayer for us today is that we give God the glory due to His name. "Give unto the LORD the glory due to His name; Worship the LORD in the beauty of holiness." Psalm 29:2

"For it is written: 'As I live, says the LORD, Every knee shall bow to Me, And every tongue shall confess to God.'" Romans 14:11

DAY 29

Why?

"Why do the nations rage, And the people plot a vain thing? The kings of the earth set themselves, And the rulers take counsel together, Against the LORD and against His Anointed, saying, "Let us break Their bonds in pieces And cast away Their cords from us." He who sits in the heavens shall laugh; The Lord shall hold them in derision. Then He shall speak to them in His wrath, And distress them in His deep displeasure:" Psalm 2:1-5

Why does a teacher ask a question that they already have the answer to the question? Yes, it's for the student to gain perspective and knowledge that will help transform their thinking.

The Psalmist seems genuinely mystified in asking the question. The questioner knows that the nations have no reason to rage against God, and they have no benefit in raging against Him. They oppose both the LORD and His Anointed. Anointed speaks of Christ, the Anointed One. Since Jesus is the perfect representation of the Father (John 10:30, 14:9) if you oppose God the Father, you oppose Jesus. If you oppose Jesus, you oppose God the Father. Therefore, their opposition against God is nothing but a vain thing.

The response to the question is that God laughs because He sits in the heavens. It isn't just an earthly throne He occupies; it is the throne of heaven with authority over all creation. In other words, what does heaven have to fear from earth?

The sad truth is that many have opposed God and His Kingdom in Jesus Christ through the centuries. However, each one of these opponents has been frustrated and crushed. Why? Because "The LORD shall hold them in derision."

My prayer for us today is that we give God the glory due to His name. "Give unto the LORD the glory due to His name; Worship the LORD in the beauty of holiness." Psalm 29:2

"For it is written: 'As I live, says the LORD, Every knee shall bow to Me, And every tongue shall confess to God.'" Romans 14:11

DAY 30

The Blessed

"Blessed is the man Who walks not in the counsel of the ungodly, Nor stands in the path of sinners, Nor sits in the seat of the scornful; But his delight is in the law of the LORD, and in His law he meditates day and night." Psalm 1:1-2

What makes a person blessed according to Psalm 1?

First, it means the "blessed" knows how to discern the counsel of the ungodly. Unfortunately, many fail at this point. They do not even consider if counsel is godly or ungodly. For example, today, many are receiving pastoral care (being shepherd) by major News Outlets.

The Psalmist reminds us that sinners have a path where they stand, and the "blessed" man knows he does not belong on that path. Path speaks of a way, a road, a direction, and the blessed person is not traveling in the same direction as those who practice sin.

Throughout the Psalms, the phrase law of the LORD describes God's entire word, not only the "law" portion of the first five books of the Bible. Thus, the "blessed" person delights in the word of God!

The blessed person meditates or ponders on the word of God. They do not just hear it and forget it but continue to think about it.

One simple way of meditating on the law (scriptures) is by carefully thinking about each word and phrase, applying it to oneself, and praying it back to the Lord.

My prayer for us today is that we live a blessed life.

DAY 31

Overcoming Intimidation

"lest Satan should take advantage of us; for we are not ignorant of his devices." 2 Corinthians 2:11

Intimidation is one of the devices of Satan. His influence can come from all different sources. For example:

INTIMIDATION FROM FAMILY: "Now Eliab, his oldest brother, heard when he spoke to the men; and Eliab's anger was aroused against David, and he said, 'Why did you come down here? And with whom have you left those few sheep in the wilderness? I know your pride and the insolence of your heart, for you have come down to see the battle.'" 1 Samuel 17:28

INTIMIDATION FROM LEADERSHIP: "And Saul said to David, 'You are not able to go against this Philistine to fight with him; for you are a youth, and he a man of war from his youth.'" 1 Samuel 17:33

INTIMIDATION FROM YOUR ENEMY: "And the Philistine said to David, 'Come to me, and I will give your flesh to the birds of the air and the beasts of the field!'" 1 Samuel 17:44

David overcame intimidation by knowing the greatness of the Shepherd: "The LORD is my shepherd; I shall not want" (Psalm 23:1).

The enemy wants to intimidate us because he wants to rob our peace, joy, and fellowship with God and His people. However, we are not ignorant of Satan's devices. Jesus has given us victory over the enemy's plot to keep us in bondage.

My prayer for us is that we would overcome intimidation today and be able to say, "But thanks be to God, who gives us the victory through our Lord Jesus Christ." 1 Corinthians 15:57

DAY 32

Shine Before All

"You are the light of the world. A city that is set on a hill cannot be hidden. Nor do they light a lamp and put it under a basket, but on a lampstand, and it gives light to all who are in the house. Let your light so shine before men, that they may see your good works and glorify your Father in heaven."
Matthew 5:14-16

Shining your Light before men has the meaning of being exposed to the view of all, openly and publicly. Therefore, when Jesus says that we are the Light of the world, He says that we are not only light-receivers but also light-givers. This appeal should lead us to an understanding of having a concern for others and not just ourselves. In other words, we cannot live only to ourselves; we must have someone to shine too and do so willingly and lovingly.

HIS Light is needed because the world is in darkness, and if our faith imitates the world's darkness, we have nothing to show. Therefore, to be effective, we must seek and display the Christian principles of faith, which is ultimately HIS light shining through us.

Remember, Jesus never challenged us to become salt or Light. Instead, he said that we are – and we are either fulfilling or falling short of that given responsibility.

My prayer for us today is to let our Light [HIS Light] so shine before men that they may see our good works and glorify our Father in heaven.

DAY 33

Rest

"Come to Me, all you who labor and are heavy laden, and I will give you rest." Matthew 11:28

"Then Jesus said, "Come to me, all of you who are weary and carry heavy burdens, and I will give you rest. Take my yoke upon you. Let me teach you, because I am humble and gentle at heart, and you will find rest for your souls. For my yoke is easy to bear, and the burden I give you is light." Matthew 11:28-30

Are you in need of rest? The Good Shepherd can lift and take away your heavy burdens.

Today I am reminded of a story that took place in New Zealand in 2004. There was a Merino sheep by the name of Shrek, and he had become quite famous. Shrek had been hiding out in caves on the South Island for six years. The owner, John Perriam, did not even seem to miss him for several years. Perriam had 17,000 Merino sheep on his ranch. They were known for their prize wool, some of the softest in the world. During these years, his fleece continued to grow. Most sheep have a fleece weighing about ten pounds that needs to be shaved (shorn) each year. Shrek's fleece weighed sixty pounds. That's enough wool to make 20 men's suits. Shrek carried this tremendous burden year after year, and it continued to grow. All because he had wandered away from his shepherd. But once he came back to his shepherd, John

Perriam, the burden was lifted. The shepherd sheared the Sheep.

Jesus, the Great Shepherd, is the One who can lift our heavyweights. It is He who can shave our fleece and take away our self-imposed burdens. So if you have wandered away from the Good Shepherd and life isn't what you want it to be, all you need to do is come to Him.

My prayer for us today is that we come into HIS rest.

DAY 34

Teaching

"Then He opened His mouth and taught them, saying:
"Blessed are..." Matthew 5:2-3

Did you ever have a teacher that you loved listening to their lecture? Most likely, if you did, it was because that teacher was imparting to you a desire to want to learn and grow.

I love reading that Jesus "opened His mouth and taught them." Jesus, the Great Rabbi, is giving His disciples instructions that will transform their lives. His teaching informs the disciples on how to live in His Everlasting Kingdom.

Jesus' teaching on the Sermon on the Mount is also known as the "Declaration of the Kingdom." The American Revolutionaries had their Declaration of Independence. Karl Marx had his Communist Manifesto. With this message, Jesus declared what His Kingdom is all about. His teaching expresses the spiritual implications of His rule in our lives. In other words, this Sermon on the Mount is teaching us how we will live when Jesus is our LORD, and HIS kingdom is established in us.

My prayer for us today is that we pray: "Your kingdom come, Your will be done, on earth as it is in heaven." Matthew 6:10

DAY 35

Those Who Mourn

"Blessed are those who mourn, For they shall be comforted."
Matthew 5:4

Why mourn? What does mourning produce? In this verse, the ancient Greek grammar indicates an intense degree of mourning. I believe this weeping is for the broken and needy condition of both the individual and society. This awareness of brokenness and neediness is the result of understanding one's sin condition. In other words, those who mourn are mourning over their sin or society's sins and their effects.

"Therefore submit to God. Resist the devil and he will flee from you. Draw near to God and He will draw near to you. Cleanse your hands, you sinners; and purify your hearts, you double-minded. Lament and mourn and weep! Let your laughter be turned to mourning and your joy to gloom. Humble yourselves in the sight of the Lord, and He will lift you up." James 4:7-10

Here is the good news, those who mourn over their sin and sinful condition come to know comfort. Remember, God allows this grief into our lives as a path, not as a destination.

"For His anger is but for a moment, His favor is for life; Weeping may endure for a night, But joy comes in the morning." Psalm 30:5

One final thought: Those who mourn can know a closeness to the Man of Sorrows who was acquainted with grief (Isaiah 53:3).

My prayer for us today is that we experience the blessing of God's comfort so that we can share that comfort with others.

DAY 36

Blessed Are The Poor In Spirit

"Blessed are the poor in spirit, For theirs is the kingdom of heaven." Matthew 5:3

What does it mean to be "blessed?" It means to be happy, fortunate, and well off. When we read these words, we can be encouraged knowing that Jesus wants us to experience this position. I call it a "position" because sometimes the condition surrounding our lives doesn't reflect blessing. However, when we understand Jesus' eternal words, we can ultimately see our inward place (soul) of gifts.

It's no coincidence that "poor in spirit" is the first of the beatitudes. This attitude is the confession God is looking for from us. It is a recognition that all have sinned and fallen short of the glory of God. The poor in spirit have no problem acknowledging their dependence on God and their need for His redemptive plan. As Spurgeon once said: "Not what I have, but what I have not, is the first point of contact, between my soul and God."

Today, I pray that we know our dependency upon Him and, most importantly, His desire to see us blessed.

DAY 37

The Meek

"Blessed are the meek, For they shall inherit the earth."
Matthew 5:5

When someone is meek, they have a mild disposition and gentleness of spirit. Meekness is the opposite of self-assertiveness and self-interest. It stems from trust in God's goodness and control over the situation. The gentle person is not occupied with themself at all. This position of humility is a work of the Holy Spirit, not of the human will. In the vocabulary of the ancient Greek language, the meek person was not passive or easily pushed around. The main idea behind the word "meek" was strength under control, like a strong stallion trained to do the job instead of running wild.

Meekness toward God is that disposition of spirit in which we accept His dealings with us as good and therefore without disputing or resisting. In the OT, the meek rely on God rather than their strength to defend against injustice. Meekness can acknowledge that God will sometimes allow evil people and nations to inflict pain and suffering. However, the meek understand that God is using all of this to purify His elect. The truth is, God will deliver His people in His perfect time (Isaiah 41:17, Luke 18:1-8).

The promise "they shall inherit the earth" proves that God will not allow His meek ones to end up on the short end of the deal.

My prayer is that we experience His meekness.

DAY 38

Hunger & Thirst

"Blessed are those who hunger and thirst for righteousness, For they shall be filled." Matthew 5:6

It is good to remember that Jesus said this in a day and a culture that understood what it means to be hungry and thirsty. Today – at least in the western world – it is hard to grasp because we have so much. People are hungering for many things: power, authority, success, comfort, happiness – but how many hunger and thirst for righteousness? For example, let us do more than just hunger and thirst that our political party may get into power. But instead, we should hunger and thirst that His righteousness may be revealed in our land. Also, we should not be hungering and thirsting for our vengeance and judgment to come but rather hungering and thirsting for His righteousness to be known.

Unfortunately, many are not walking in the blessings that God intended because of the development of bad cravings and eating habits (spiritually thinking).

Jesus promised to fill the hungry, to fill them with as much as they long to be filled. The filling is a beautiful promise that both satisfies us and keeps us longing for more.

My prayer is that we know the blessing of being filled as we hunger and thirst for His righteousness.

DAY 39

Merciful

"Blessed are the merciful, For they shall obtain mercy."
Matthew 5:7

The Greek word for merciful is ἐλεέω. It is only found one other time in the New Testament. The second time is in Hebrews 2:17 "Therefore, in all things He had to be made like His brethren, that He might be a merciful and faithful High Priest in things pertaining to God, to make propitiation for the sins of the people."

It is evident in this 2nd verse that Jesus is the Merciful One. It is because of His mercy that we can be saved. It is because of His mercy that we can become merciful. I love the words found in Lamentations 3:21-23 "This I recall to my mind; therefore I have hope. Through the LORD's mercies, we are not consumed, Because His compassions fail not. They are new every morning; Great is Your faithfulness." To simply put it, if we want mercy, we should be merciful to others. Some people wonder why God showed such remarkable mercy to King David, especially in the terrible ways in which he sinned. One reason God gave him such compassion was because David was notably merciful to many different individuals. For example, David towards King Saul was kind on several occasions to a very unworthy Saul. In David, the merciful obtained mercy.

Today, my prayer is to experience a blessed life by being a channel of God's mercy towards others.

72

DAY 40

Pure In Heart

"Blessed are the pure in heart, For they shall see God."
Matthew 5:8

A biblical definition of pure is the following:

A. physically
    1. purified by fire
    2. in a similitude, like a vine cleansed by pruning and so
fitted   to bear fruit

B. Ethically
    1. free from corrupt desire, sin, and guilt
    2. free from every mixture of what is false, sincere,
    genuine
    3. blameless, innocent
    4. unstained with the guilt of anything

Know this, the pure of heart receive the most beautiful
reward. The pure will enjoy greater intimacy with God than
they could have imagined. However, the polluting sins of
covetousness, oppression, lust and the love of money all have
a definite blinding effect upon a person; the one pure of heart
is free from these pollutions.

Ultimately, this intimate relationship with God must become
our most significant motivation for purity, greater than a fear
of getting caught or a fear of consequences.

"But the wisdom that is from above is first pure, then peaceable, gentle, willing to yield, full of mercy and good fruits, without partiality and without hypocrisy." James 3:17

My prayer for us today is that we are blessed with purity so that what we see is filled with faith, hope, and love. "And now abide faith, hope, love, these three; but the greatest of these is love." 1 Corinthians 13:13

DAY 41

Peacemakers

"Blessed are the peacemakers, For they shall be called sons of God." Matthew 5:9

It can be very lonely living without peace. Even worse than being lonely are the overwhelming feelings of anger, bitterness, and guilt. The lack of peace can destroy us from the inside to the out. This discontentment is ultimately the devil's plot, to kill, steal, and destroy (see John 10:10).

Those who bring about peace are those who have learned how to overcome evil with good. We accomplish this by spreading the Gospel because God has entrusted the ministry of reconciliation (2 Corinthians 5:18). In sharing the Gospel (the good news of Jesus), we make peace between man and the God whom they have rejected and offended.

For they shall be called sons of God: The reward of the peacemakers is that they are recognized as true children of God. Why? Because they share His passion for peace and reconciliation, the breaking down of walls between people.

"For He Himself is our peace, who has made both one, and has broken down the middle wall of separation, having abolished in His flesh the enmity, that is, the law of commandments contained in ordinances, so as to create in Himself one new man from the two, thus making peace, and that He might reconcile them both to God in one body through the cross, thereby putting to death the enmity. And

75

He came and preached peace to you who were afar off and to those who were near. For through Him we both have access by one Spirit to the Father." Ephesians 2:14-18

My prayer for us today is that we receive His peace today to be peacemakers and know the joy of being HIS child.

DAY 42

Those Who Are Persecuted

*"Blessed are those who are persecuted for righteousness'
sake, For theirs is the kingdom of heaven. Blessed are you
when they revile and persecute you, and say all kinds of evil
against you falsely for My sake. Rejoice and be exceedingly
glad, for great is your reward in heaven, for so they
persecuted the prophets who were before you." Matthew
5:10-12*

It's important to note that those blessed are persecuted for
righteousness sake and Jesus's sake (for My sake), not for
their stupidity or self-centered views. Peter recognized that
suffering might come to some Christians for reasons other
than their faithfulness to Jesus when he said, "If you are
reproached for the name of Christ, blessed are you, for the
Spirit of glory and of God rests upon you. On their part He is
blasphemed, but on your part He is glorified. But let none of
you suffer as a murderer, a thief, an evildoer, or as a busybody
in other people's matters" (1Peter 4:14-15).

In the book of Acts, we read that it did not take long for these
words of Jesus to ring true to His followers. Early Christians
heard many enemies say all kinds of evil against them falsely
for Jesus' sake. However, Jesus was lifting the disciple's
vision when He said, "Rejoice and be exceedingly glad." This
phrase could translate to say that the persecuted should "leap
for joy." Why? Because the persecuted will have a great
reward in heaven, and the oppressed are in good company:
the prophets before them were also persecuted.

77

My prayer for us today: "Beloved, I beg you as sojourners and pilgrims, abstain from fleshly lusts which war against the soul, having your conduct honorable among the Gentiles, that when they speak against you as evildoers, they may, by your good works which they observe, glorify God in the day of visitation." 1 Peter 2:11-12

DAY 43

You Are The Salt Of The Earth

"You are the salt of the earth; but if the salt loses its flavor, how shall it be seasoned? It is then good for nothing but to be thrown out and trampled underfoot by men." Matthew 5:13

In Jesus' day, salt was a valued commodity. Roman soldiers were sometimes paid with salt, introducing the phrase "worth his salt." The disciples of Jesus were called to be like salt because they have a preserving influence. In that day, salt was used to preserve meats and slow decay. So, Christians should have a preserving impact on their culture. Having salt was also symbolized by having wisdom and grace exhibited in your speech. Salt must keep its "saltiness" to be of any value or usefulness. When it is no good as salt, it is trampled underfoot. In the same way, the Christian is admonished not to lose their "flavor" and so become good for nothing. This appeal is one of the reasons James records these words: "If anyone among you thinks he is religious, and does not bridle his tongue but deceives his own heart, this one's religion is useless." James 1:26

My prayer for us today is that we remain salty in these difficult times.

DAY 44

Every Day

"I will extol You, my God, O King; And I will bless Your name forever and ever. Every day I will bless You, And I will praise Your name forever and ever." Psalm 145:1-2

What you do every day reveals who you are and what is a priority in your life. The truth is, no one knows what we will face every day in the year ahead. However, we can choose that no matter how difficult or exciting the days ahead will be, we can acknowledge our need to praise our God as King. Praising God must be our daily work. No day should pass that we don't bless His name. Just like our dependency on air in our lungs, we cannot experience true life without His name being praised through our lips, forever and ever.

The Psalmist recognized that God is blessing us every day with the provision of life, light, and hope. Therefore, it is only fitting that we should be every day blessing Him and giving Him honor.

My prayer for us today is: "So He said to them, "When you pray, say: Our Father in heaven, Hallowed be Your name. Your kingdom come. Your will be done On earth as it is in heaven. Give us day by day our daily bread." Luke 11:2-3

DAY 45

His Greatness Is Unsearchable

"Great is the LORD, and greatly to be praised; And His greatness is unsearchable." Psalm 145:3

Why is God's greatness unsearchable? Simply put, because HIS praise can never be stopped. Eternity will reveal how Great the LORD is and how greatly He is to be praised. But, unfortunately, I have witnessed many former and wounded believers who have swallowed the lies of the enemy. They were fooled into thinking that they knew all the ways of God and replaced His endless praise with jealousy, complaining, and bitterness.

The Prophet Isaiah proclaimed this question: "Have you not known? Have you not heard? The everlasting God, the LORD, The Creator of the ends of the earth, Neither faints nor is weary. His understanding is unsearchable." Isaiah 40:28

The Apostle Paul also considers God's greatness, and he breaks into spontaneous praise. He says in Romans 11:33, "Oh, the depth of the riches both of the wisdom and knowledge of God! How unsearchable are His judgments and His ways past finding out!" Paul realizes that God's ways are past finding out, and God's wisdom and knowledge are beyond him.

My prayer for us today is that we would never stop giving the LORD the praise due to His name: "I will extol You, my God,

O King; And I will bless Your name forever and ever. Every day I will bless You, And I will praise Your name forever and ever." Psalm 145:1-2

DAY 46

I Will Meditate

"I will meditate on the glorious splendor of Your majesty, And on Your wondrous works." Psalm 145:5

What does it mean to meditate? The Hebrew word that we translate "meditate" is שִׂיחַ. It means to put forth, mediate, muse, commune, speak, complain, ponder, sing. For those of us who write songs, it is through meditation that the song is birthed and comes to life.

The more significant question we need to ask ourselves for the coming days is, "what will we meditate on?" The Psalmist gives us the proper focus, and it is the glorious splendor of HIS majesty and HIS wondrous works.

This coming year we will experience obstacles, distractions, and deception, but for those of us who choose to meditate on HIS Word, we will be ready to give an answer for our hope: "But sanctify the Lord God in your hearts, and always be ready to give a defense to everyone who asks you a reason for the hope that is in you, with meekness and fear;" 1 Peter 3:15

My prayer for us today is that we would be filled with songs of praise so that no matter what we may see or experience, we have hope.

DAY 47

Speak

"Men shall speak of the might of Your awesome acts, And I will declare Your greatness. Psalm 145:6

I love speaking about the great acts of Jesus. How he turned the water to wine, healed the blind, raised the dead, and how HE showed compassion to the multitudes. I love reading how Peter became bold to speak about Jesus: "Then Peter opened his mouth and said: "In truth, I perceive that God shows no partiality. But in every nation, whoever fears Him and works righteousness is accepted by Him. The word which God sent to the children of Israel, preaching peace through Jesus Christ — He is Lord of all— that word you know, which was proclaimed throughout all Judea, and began from Galilee after the baptism which John preached: how God anointed Jesus of Nazareth with the Holy Spirit and with power, who went about doing good and healing all who were oppressed by the devil, for God was with Him." Acts 10:34-38

The scriptures also remind us: "A good man out of the good treasure of his heart brings forth good; and an evil man out of the evil treasure of his heart brings forth evil. For out of the abundance of the heart his mouth speaks." Luke 6:45

My prayer for us today is that our hearts are filled with God's greatness so that what we speak throughout the day reflects that.

DAY 48

Memory

"They shall utter the memory of Your great goodness, And shall sing of Your righteousness." Psalm 145:7

When I was ten years old, I was involved in a motorcycle collision. As a result of the accident, I was hospitalized for over a week with total loss of memory. It's a bizarre feeling to have lost memory and then listen to others describe what took place in your life.

The Psalmist reminds us of the importance of uttering God's goodness. He wants us to keep the memories of His goodness alive in our hearts. But, unfortunately, the truth is, we have an enemy of our soul who would like to cause us to have accidents so that we would lose the memory of God's "great goodness." The Psalmist also reminds us of the importance of singing of HIS righteousness and how singing is meant to be from the heart. Many who can't sing a beautiful melody with the voice can still have a beautiful sound in their heart: "speaking to one another in psalms and hymns and spiritual songs, singing and making melody in your heart to the Lord," Ephesians 5:19

My prayer for us today is that our hearts would be filled with the WORD of GOD so that our memories of HIS great goodness would cause us to sing.

DAY 49

Full of Compassion

"The LORD is gracious and full of compassion, Slow to anger and great in mercy." Psalm 145:8

When I read what the LORD is "full of," it makes me want to pray to be filled the same. Compassion is beautiful to witness and even more amazing to experience when you are in need.

I love reading Psalm 145 as we learn how the Lord is gracious to those that serve him; He is full of compassion to those that need Him, slow to anger to those that have offended Him, and of great mercy to all that seek Him. The good news is that He is "full of compassion," so He is ready to give and ready to forgive. First, however, we must turn to Him. The scriptures also remind us that "Love suffereth long and is kind," and God is love. "In other words, it is because of His love that He is slow to anger. So we read in 2 Peter 3:9, "The Lord is not slack concerning His promise, as some count slackness, but is long-suffering toward us, not willing that any should perish but that all should come to repentance."

It is beautiful to read that the LORD is slow to anger and great in mercy.

My prayer for us today is that we are "full" of what God's love reveals and not what the world demonstrates.

DAY 50

The LORD is Good to All

"The Lord is good to all: and his tender mercies are over all his works." Psalm 145:9

Does "all" really mean all? I heard someone say once, "For God so loved the world (John 3:16), doesn't mean some people." In other words, their thinking goes like this; God limits His love and mercy to only a specific group of people. I find this thinking disturbing, and even worse, I believe the devil and his demons drive it. The devil would love to give people an excuse to hate and despise. It should be grievous for us to see people become merciless in their speech, because unfortunately, when they speak like this, they fall right into the hands of the enemy's plot. The plot of the enemy has always been to limit and even diminish the works of God. This evil plan is another reason why it is essential to declare, like the Psalmist, these powerful words: "The Lord is good to all: and his tender mercies are over all his works." May God help us to proclaim the right message in the day and hour that we live.

My prayer for us today is: "Men shall speak of the might of Your awesome acts, And I will declare Your greatness. They shall utter the memory of Your great goodness, And shall sing of Your righteousness. The LORD is gracious and full of compassion, Slow to anger and great in mercy." Psalm 145:6-8

DAY 51

Your Saints Shall Bless You

"All Your works shall praise You, O LORD, And Your saints shall bless You. They shall speak of the glory of Your kingdom, And talk of Your power, To make known to the sons of men His mighty acts, And the glorious majesty of His kingdom. Your kingdom is an everlasting kingdom, And Your dominion endures throughout all generations." Psalm 145:10-13

This Psalm reveals some of the ways the Saints will bless the LORD.

1. They speak of the glory of His kingdom.
2. They talk of His power.
3. They make known to people His mighty acts.
4. They make known an everlasting Kingdom and a King that rules throughout all generations.

When the Saints of God are blessing their King, they're not drawn away by the things Paul talks about in Ephesians 5:3-4 "....let it not even be named among you, as is fitting for saints; neither filthiness, nor foolish talking, nor coarse jesting, which are not fitting, but rather giving of thanks."

My prayer for us today comes from the testimony of a Gentile king and how God changed his heart: "I thought it good to declare the signs and wonders that the Most High God has worked for me. How great are His signs, And how mighty His wonders! His kingdom is an everlasting kingdom, And His dominion is from generation to generation." Daniel 4:2-3

DAY 52

Upholds All Who Fall

"The LORD upholds all who fall, And raises up all who are bowed down." Psalm 145:14

What do you see in this verse? I believe we can see the very heart of God. His love to rescue, pick up and strengthen the weak. The Psalmist David said it this way in Psalm 37: "Though he fall, he shall not be utterly cast down; For the LORD upholds him with His hand" (Psalm 37:24). Truth be known, God is the very strength of our life. He is the One who raises us and gives us what we need.

When we see the very heart of God, we can say, like David in Psalm 27:1, "The LORD is my light and my salvation; Whom shall I fear? The LORD is the strength of my life; Of whom shall I be afraid?"

We can also declare: "God is our refuge and strength, A very present help in trouble. Therefore we will not fear, Even though the earth be removed, And though the mountains be carried into the midst of the sea; Though its waters roar and be troubled, Though the mountains shake with its swelling. Selah" Psalm 46:1-3

My prayer for us today is that we know that God is there for us even if we stumble or fall.

DAY 53

Satisfy The Desire

"The eyes of all look expectantly to You, And You give them their food in due season. You open Your hand And satisfy the desire of every living thing." Psalm 145:15-16

Wow! Did you read that? It is the hand of God that satisfies our desire. Ok, what does it mean to satisfy the desire, you might ask. It has to do with pleasure, delight, favor, goodwill, acceptance, and self-will. Desire is God-given but can only be beneficial when it is received and fulfilled from the hand of God. Therefore, recognizing God's provision, protection, and power is vital if we are going to live a satisfying life.

What are your desires? How will you see these desires fulfilled?

My prayer for us today is from Psalm 37:4-5 "Delight yourself also in the LORD, And He shall give you the desires of your heart. Commit your way to the LORD, Trust also in Him, And He shall bring it to pass."

DAY 54

Righteous & Gracious

"The LORD is righteous in all His ways, Gracious in all His works." Psalm 145:17

When I think about the LORD and how righteous and gracious He is, I am immediately reminded of the story of Job. In the book of Job, we read about his suffering and pain, but his problem goes far beyond his physical, social, and financial difficulties. Job must deal with the fact that God does not always act the way he thought God would and should work in his life. His conclusion is this: "Then Job answered the LORD and said: 'I know that You can do everything and that no purpose of Yours can be withheld from You.' You asked, 'Who is this who hides counsel without knowledge?' Therefore I have uttered what I did not understand, Things too wonderful for me, which I did not know. Listen, please, and let me speak; You said, 'I will question you, and you shall answer Me.' 'I have heard of You by the hearing of the ear, But now my eye sees You. Therefore I abhor myself, And repent in dust and ashes.'" Job 42:1-6

Like the Psalmist & Job, we need to understand that God wants to give us an encounter with Him. An experience where we see how HE is righteous in all HIS ways and gracious in all His works.

My prayer for us today is: "Show me Your ways, O LORD; Teach me Your paths. Lead me in Your truth and teach me,

For You are the God of my salvation; On You I wait all the day." Psalm 25:4-5

DAY 55

Fulfill The Desire

"The LORD is near to all who call upon Him, To all who call upon Him in truth. He will fulfill the desire of those who fear Him; He also will hear their cry and save them." Psalm 145:18-19

Where do your desires come from in your life? Where does your cry come from in your life? Most would say, from deep within the heart. Others say it is from deep within the soul, consisting of your mind, will, and emotions. Our desires and cries will affect us in our bodies, souls, and spirits. Therefore, what we desire and to whom we cry out is very significant. The Psalmist is reminding us that God will hear those who fear (reverence, worship) Him. He will listen to their call and will save them; that is, hearing them as he heard David (that is, saved him) in Psalm 22:20-21 - "Deliver Me from the sword, My precious life from the power of the dog. Save Me from the lion's mouth And from the horns of the wild oxen! You have answered Me."

The answer is God fulfilling your desires and hearing your cry. He is delivering those who fear Him and call upon Him in truth.

Today, my prayer is that God would place His desires and truth in our hearts. "Into Your hand, I commit my spirit; You have redeemed me, O LORD God of truth." Psalm 31:5

94

DAY 56

The LORD Preserves

"The LORD preserves all who love Him, But all the wicked He will destroy." Psalm 145:20

Reading this verse, I walk away with some important conclusions:

#1 Love will be preserved;
#2 Wickedness will be destroyed.

The word "preserves" in Hebrew - שָׁמַר translated shâmar, (pronounced shaw-mar'). It is a primitive root, meaning: properly, to hedge about (as with thorns), i.e., guard; generally, to protect, attend to, or to watch. Simply put, those who receive God's love will be watched and protected. On the other hand, we read the wicked will be destroyed. The word wicked in Hebrew is רָשָׁע translated râshâ' (pronounced raw-shaw'). It means morally wrong; concretely, an (actively) bad person:— condemned, guilty, ungodly, wicked (man), that did wrong. The Bible is clear that God will eventually destroy, eliminate, and exterminate the wicked. In other words, God will preserve those who love Him, even by destroying the wicked that would cause harm to His people.

My prayer for us today is this we know the power of God's love to preserve us: "But the transgressors shall be destroyed together; The future of the wicked shall be cut off. But the salvation of the righteous is from the LORD; He is their strength in the time of trouble. And the LORD shall help them

95

and deliver them; He shall deliver them from the wicked, And save them, Because they trust in Him." Psalm 37:38-40

DAY 57

My Mouth Shall Speak

"My mouth shall speak the praise of the LORD, And all flesh shall bless His holy name Forever and ever." Psalm 145:21

The Psalmist concludes by making this powerful statement in what he chooses to speak:

He chooses to speak praise to the LORD.
He chooses to speak exhortation for all flesh to bless the LORD forever and ever.

Speech is powerful and what we do with it has consequences. For example, we read in scripture: "Death and life are in the power of the tongue, And those who love it will eat its fruit." Proverbs 18:21

In the scriptures, we are also reminded where our speech comes from: "A good man out of the good treasure of his heart brings forth good; and an evil man out of the evil treasure of his heart brings forth evil. For out of the abundance of the heart, his mouth speaks" Luke 6:45. The bottom line is this: we will all choose our final destiny by what we allow to fill our hearts and ultimately come forth from our lips.

My prayer for us today is that while we still have breath to draw, may our mouths speak God's praises. "Uphold my steps in Your paths, That my footsteps may not slip. I have called upon You, for You will hear me, O God; Incline Your ear to me, and hear my speech." Psalm 17:5-6

DAY 58

Give Every Day

"Give, and it will be given to you: good measure, pressed down, shaken together, and running over will be put into your bosom. For with the same measure that you use, it will be measured back to you." Luke 6:38

Do you want to live a blessed life? Give something away every day this coming year. Don't ever stop giving.

Jesus encouraged the freedom to live without fear. He wanted us to be set free from the fear of giving too much. The truth is, you can't out-give God. He will return more to you, in one way or another, more than you give to Him. Yet, the most pointed application of this in context is not so much the giving of material resources but with showing love, grace, and forgiveness. We are never the loser when we provide those things after the pattern of God's heart of generosity.

My prayer for us today is this: "Cause me to hear Your lovingkindness in the morning, For in You do I trust; Cause me to know the way in which I should walk, For I lift up my soul to You." Psalm 143:8

DAY 59

In The Morning

"Give ear to my words, O LORD, Consider my meditation. Give heed to the voice of my cry, My King and my God, For to You I will pray. My voice You shall hear in the morning, O LORD; In the morning I will direct it to You, And I will look up." Psalm 5:1-3

It is 6:00 on an early March morning, and as I look out the window, it is still dark. Yet, despite it still being dark, I have anticipation that the Sun is coming soon.

David prayed to his King, the LORD, in the morning. It says of him that, "I will look up." Strong's Definitions: צָפָה tsâphâh; a primitive root; properly, to lean forward, i.e., to peer into the distance; by implication, to observe, await:— behold, espy, lookup (well), wait for, (keep the) watch(-man). David gives us what to do before and after prayer. Before we pray, we should direct our prayer. The idea behind direct is not "to aim" but "to order, to arrange. In other words, it's intentional, personal, and deliberate. After we pray, we look up with expectancy to heaven, really believing that God will answer. This prayer is where true hope comes from in our lives.

"Let holy preparation link hands with patient expectation, and we shall have far larger answers to our prayers." (Spurgeon)

My prayer for us today is that we direct our focus to the King and keep looking up.

DAY 60

The Scriptures Testify Of JESUS

"You search the Scriptures, for in them you think you have eternal life; and these are they which testify of Me. But you are not willing to come to Me that you may have life." John 5:39-40

The religious leaders in Jesus' day rejected Him because they rejected God's word through Moses. In other words, they did not believe the testimony of Moses because they turned away from what he wrote about Jesus, the coming Messiah.

"For if you believed Moses, you would believe Me; for he wrote about Me. But if you do not believe his writings, how will you believe My words?" John 5:46-47

Jesus said of the Scriptures that they testify of Me (John 5:39). Here are seven examples:

The Lord, your God, will raise up for you a Prophet like me from your midst, from your brethren. Him you shall hear. (Deuteronomy 18:15 & Acts 3:22-26)
"And as Moses lifted up the serpent in the wilderness, even so must the Son of Man be lifted up," John 3:14 & Numbers 21:8-9)
Jesus is symbolized in the rock that gave Israel water in the wilderness (Numbers 20:8-12 and 1 Corinthians 10:4).
The ministry of Jesus is shown in almost every aspect of the seven different kinds of offering that God commanded Israel to bring (Leviticus 1-7 & Ephesians 5:2).

101

Jesus and His ministry is shown in the Tabernacle and its service. One place where the New Testament makes this connection is with the word propitiation in Romans 3:25, which speaks of the mercy seat on the Ark of the Covenant. The law of the bondservant speaks of Jesus (Exodus 21:5-6 and Psalm 40:6-8).

Jesus was giving a Bible study on the Road to Emmaus "...beginning at Moses and all the Prophets, He expounded to them in all the Scriptures the things concerning Himself (Luke 24:27).

My prayer for us today is that we believe the words of Moses, who prophetically declared: that Jesus is the Messiah, the Son of God, and God the Son.

DAY 61

Radiant Joy

"They looked to Him and were radiant, And their faces were not ashamed." Psalms 34:5 NKJV

The word "looked" in Hebrew is נָבַט. The transliteration is *nabat*. Looked is defined as the following:

1. To look
2. To regard, show regard to, pay attention to, consider
3. To look upon, regard, show regard to

What you "look" to is very important because it influences your life. The Psalmist declares that those who look towards the LORD will find life, light, liberty, love, and everything they need, so they are not put to shame. "And their faces were not ashamed." Again, those who looked to the LORD were covered with joy because they looked to the LORD. Unfortunately, people don't realize the danger of looking to the wrong source. For example: "But his wife looked back behind him, and she became a pillar of salt." Genesis 19:26

My prayer for us today is that our faces would be radiant with joy.

DAY 62

Stumble

"But whoever causes one of these little ones who believe in Me to stumble, it would be better for him if a millstone were hung around his neck, and he were thrown into the sea."
Mark 9:42

Causing people to stumble and being offended can be an everyday occurrence in the political and social environment we live in today. However, being the "cause" of people stumbling is something Jesus spoke very critical of: it would be better for him if a millstone were hung around his neck, and he were thrown into the sea.

Jesus also said, at another time, that it was impossible for the offenses not to come (Matthew 18:7). That being said, how does one guard against offending and being offended? The answer is found in the scriptures: "Great peace have those who love Your law, And nothing causes them to stumble" (Psalm 119:165). Understanding that Jesus Christ is the fulfillment of the Law, we can conclude that those who love Jesus will experience "Great Peace" amid the turmoil and a hostile environment. The opposite is true; when you don't know who Jesus is, you are vulnerable for the offense to come: "Is this not the carpenter, the Son of Mary, and brother of James, Joses, Judas, and Simon? And are not His sisters here with us?" So they were offended at Him." Mark 6:3

Remember the story of Peter walking on water with Jesus (Matthew 14:28-30)? As long as Peter kept his eyes on Jesus, he was safe, but when he took his eyes off Jesus, he began to sink.

My prayer for us today is: "My son, let them not depart from your eyes— Keep sound wisdom and discretion; So they will be life to your soul And grace to your neck. Then you will walk safely in your way, And your foot will not stumble." Proverbs 3:21-23

DAY 63

Help In The Battle

"Asa called out to the LORD his God, saying, 'O LORD, there is no one besides You to help in the battle between the powerful and the weak; so help us, O LORD our God, for we trust in and rely on You, and in Your name we have come against this multitude. O LORD, You are our God; let not man prevail against You.'" 2 Chronicles 14:11 AMP

Have you ever been in a fight you felt you could not win? You are not alone. This passage of scripture is a prayerful plea for God to fight the battle for King Asa. He was making it clear, "If they come against us, they are coming against You, God. And if they prevail against us, they have prevailed against You." Such a bold and daring way of putting the responsibility on God was reminiscent of King David's faith when he ran towards the giant Goliath, declaring, "The battle is the LORD's, and He will give you into our hands!"

Just as Asa cried out to the LORD his God in prayer, we too must correctly understand that God's power is not enhanced or limited by man's apparent strength or weakness. We should recognize that the battle belongs to the LORD and call upon God to defend His honor (do not let man prevail against You!). We, too, can trust and rely on HIM.

My prayer for us today is that we know this truth: "The horse is prepared for the day of battle, But deliverance and victory belong to the LORD." Proverb 21:31 AMP

106

DAY 64

Given You An Example

"If I then, your Lord and Teacher, have washed your feet, you also ought to wash one another's feet. For I have given you an example, that you should do as I have done to you." John 13:14-15

Who is an excellent example in your life? I dear say that their model shows you characteristics of a loving servant of people.

In the gospel writings, we learn how Jesus' entire life was a model and example to His disciples. Here He felt it was important to specifically draw attention to the lesson of what He had just done. The washing of their feet meant something, and Jesus would impart a vision for ministry in the hearts of the disciples.

We, like the disciples, would gladly wash the feet of Jesus. But He tells us to wash one another's feet. In other words, anything we do for each other that washes away the grime of the world, and the dust of defeat and the discouragement is foot washing.

Jesus certainly was an example to those disciples and all who would follow Him. Therefore, we must receive Jesus' words as an example for both attitude and action.

My prayer for us today is that we hear the words of Jesus: "Most assuredly, I say to you, a servant is not greater than his master; nor is he who is sent greater than he who sent him. If you know these things, blessed are you if you do them." John 13:16-17

DAY 65

From A Mess To A Mission

"And now I urge you to take heart, for there will be no loss of life among you, but only of the ship. For there stood by me this night an angel of the God to whom I belong and whom I serve, saying, 'Do not be afraid, Paul; you must be brought before Caesar; and indeed God has granted you all those who sail with you.' Therefore take heart, men, for I believe God that it will be just as it was told me. However, we must run aground on a certain island.'" Acts 27:22-26

The Island of Malta experienced revival and healing as a result of:

1. Paul being shipwrecked
2, Paul being bit by a snake
3. Paul responded to a need for Publius (his father was lying in   bed afflicted with a fever - Acts 28:7-8).

In chapter 28, we see that God healed Publius' father; yet it happened through the willingness and activity of Paul. God did the work, but Paul made himself ready and available for service. This experience was a great blessing and a solid contrast to the misery of the previous two weeks at sea.

The story for Paul, Luke, and Aristarchus is this: God can take what seems like a mistake and turn it around for a message of hope and healing. In other words, our life is a message in the making if we can remain open to God who does miracles.

My prayer for us today is that we would be able to see how God has turned some of our messes into a mission and message of grace and glory.

DAY 66

Jesus said... I am the Door

"Then Jesus said to them again, "Most assuredly, I say to you, I am the door of the sheep. All who ever came before Me are thieves and robbers, but the sheep did not hear them. I am the door. If anyone enters by Me, he will be saved, and will go in and out and find pasture. The thief does not come except to steal, and to kill, and to destroy. I have come that they may have life, and that they may have it more abundantly." John 10:7-10

Have you ever had to go up to a door, but you weren't sure if you were at the right house? It happened to me one time when I was trying to find someone's home. My GPS said I was there, but the house didn't seem to match the description I was looking for that day. So I drove by the house twice and finally decided to knock on the door. I was greatly relieved when my friend answered the door.

In John 10, you have a beautiful recording of the Words of Jesus. He is reminding His disciples that HE is the door to salvation. When you recognize the right door (Jesus), thieves and robbers (devil & demons) won't be able to deceive you. Thief implies deception and trickery; robber implies violence and destruction. These take away life, but Jesus gives life, and He gives it abundantly.

Jesus seems to say that His sheep are evident because they will not hear (follow after) the voice of the thieves and robbers who come after the sheep. Jesus has come to give us abundant life. Abundantly life has everything to do with relationships, trust, peace, and protection.

My prayer for us today is that we would walk through the door God has provided for us. "Jesus said to him, "I am the way, the truth, and the life. No one comes to the Father except through Me." John 14:6

DAY 67

The Armor of God

"Therefore take up the whole armor of God, that you may be able to withstand in the evil day, and having done all, to stand." Ephesians 6:13

We live in a day when it is critical that believers know what they believe and that what they follow is firmly based on the Word of God, the Bible. But, unfortunately, so many believers today are enlisting in the army of the Lord without the sword of the Spirit, and they find themselves unarmed when it comes to doing spiritual battle.

Paul introduced the idea of the whole armor of God back in Ephesians 6:11. In the following passage, he details the specific items related to the armor of God. But, first, we must understand that without the strength of God and the protection of spiritual armor, it is impossible to stand against the attacks of spiritual enemies.

Secondly, we need to understand the purpose for the strength of God and the armor of God. It is this: That you may be able to withstand in the evil day and having done all, to stand.

My prayer for us today is that we put on the armor God that has been given us in Jesus Christ. It is in His name that we will stand.

DAY 68

Do Not Be Afraid

"Now there were in the same country shepherds living out in the fields, keeping watch over their flock by night. And behold, an angel of the Lord stood before them, and the glory of the Lord shone around them, and they were greatly afraid. Then the angel said to them, 'Do not be afraid, for behold, I bring you good tidings of great joy which will be to all people. For there is born to you this day in the city of David a Savior, who is Christ the Lord. And this will be the sign to you: You will find a Babe wrapped in swaddling cloths, lying in a manger.' And suddenly there was with the angel a multitude of the heavenly host praising God and saying: 'Glory to God in the highest, And on earth peace, goodwill toward men!'" Luke 2:8-14 NKJV

This angel brought good tidings (literally, it means that they preached the gospel) to these shepherds. The reason the angel said, "Do not be afraid, " was the fact that the shepherds were filled with fear at this powerful and supernatural appearance. With this type of fear gripping their hearts, it only made the good news even sweeter.

After the single angel's announcement, a whole group of angels appeared. This appearance was the heavenly host praising God and proclaiming peace. What the world needed then was peace; what the world needs now is peace. Fear continues to fill hearts and lives today, but this same proclamation needs to be heard today: Glory to God in the highest, And on earth peace, goodwill toward men!

114

My prayer for us today is: "And the peace of God [that peace which reassures the heart, that peace] which transcends all understanding, [that peace which] stands guard over your hearts, and your minds in Christ Jesus [is yours]." Philippians 4:7 AMP

DAY 69

God's Eternal Plan

"Therefore we do not lose heart. Even though our outward man is perishing, yet the inward man is being renewed day by day. For our light affliction, which is but for a moment, is working for us a far more exceeding and eternal weight of glory, while we do not look at the things which are seen, but at the things which are not seen. For the things which are seen are temporary, but the things which are not seen are eternal." 2 Corinthians 4:16-18

How do we not lose heart in the day and hour that we live? It is essential to see that the "Therefore" is part of the answer because it points us back to what Paul just wrote. Paul began the chapter (2 Corithians 4:1) by declaring that since we have this ministry, we do not lose heart as we have received mercy. Then in the chapter, he described all the death-like sufferings he had to endure in the ministry. It is as if Paul now anticipates the question, "how can you not lose heart?"

When Paul writes "our light affliction," some might wonder if he ever knew any "real" trials. Some might even think, "Well Paul, your affliction might be light, but mine isn't. However, Paul described some of his suffering with these terms in 2 Corinthians 11:23-28: Stripes, Prisons, Beaten, Stoned, Shipwrecked, Perils of waters, Robbers, In perils from my countrymen, In perils of the Gentiles, In perils in the city, In perils in the wilderness, In perils in the sea, In perils among false brethren, In weariness and toil, In sleeplessness often, In hunger and thirst, In fastings often, In cold and nakedness.

116

Another reason why Paul does not lose heart is that his inward man was renewed day by day.

Why is our affliction light and not heavy? Because even the worst of it, by the measure of eternity, is but for a moment. Why is our affliction light and not heavy? Because of what God accomplishes in us through our affliction: a far more exceeding and eternal weight of glory.

It isn't easy to appreciate the weight of glory because it is an eternal weight. So often, the problem isn't so much in what we think about our light affliction but that the world, the flesh, and the devil want us to devalue our coming weight of glory.

Today, my prayer is that we see God's eternal plan as something beautiful and worth proclaiming like Paul.

DAY 70

A Great Mystery

"For we are members of His body, of His flesh and of His bones. "For this reason a man shall leave his father and mother and be joined to his wife, and the two shall become one flesh." This is a great mystery, but I speak concerning Christ and the church. Nevertheless let each one of you in particular so love his own wife as himself, and let the wife see that she respects her husband." Ephesians 5:30-33

These verses touch on the mystical union between Jesus and the church and its relation to marriage. Also, the marriage relationship speaks to us about the relationship between Jesus and His people. Paul quoted this essential passage from Genesis 2:24. It would be easy to think that this passage (also quoted by Jesus in Matthew 19:5) only speaks about marriage. However, Paul wants us to know that it also speaks about the relationship between Christ and the church.

Four thoughts that I formed this morning:
   1. Marriage is a picture of God's plan.
   2. Marriage helps us understand HIS desire for
   fellowship and relationship. It shows us that Jesus wants us to   be one with His Church. In other words, it shows us that Jesus   wants more than just an external, surface relationship.
   3. Marriage is a reminder that God is a covenant keeping God.
   4. Having a strong godly marriage will indicate that you do not   take Christ's sacrifice in vain.

118

My prayer for us today is that we see God's desire for unity and oneness.

DAY 71

What To Rejoice In

"Love suffers long and is kind; love does not envy; love does not parade itself, is not puffed up; does not behave rudely, does not seek its own, is not provoked, thinks no evil; **does not rejoice in iniquity, but rejoices in the truth***;" 1 Corinthians 13:4-6*

What we find ourselves rejoicing in, or over, tells us a lot about our character. Let's look at another verse that talks about what "not" to rejoice over:

"Do not rejoice when your enemy falls, And do not let your heart be glad when he stumbles; Lest the LORD see it, and it displease Him, And He turn away His wrath from him." Proverbs 24:17-18

It's very clear from these passages of scripture that God wants to teach us what is "not" worth rejoicing over. However, it's not enough to know what we are "not" to rejoice in; we also need to learn what God delights in and do the same thing. In other words, what does God want us to rejoice over? What moves His heart into rejoicing?

"And when he comes home, he calls together his friends and neighbors, saying to them, 'Rejoice with me, for I have found my sheep which was lost!' I say to you that likewise there will be more joy in heaven over one sinner who repents than over ninety-nine just persons who need no repentance. Luke 15:6-7

"Likewise, I say to you, there is joy in the presence of the angels of God over one sinner who repents." Luke 15:10

"It was right that we should make merry and be glad, for your brother was dead and is alive again, and was lost and is found." Luke 15:32

My prayer for us today is that we learn to rejoice in what God rejoices in - sinners repenting and coming home.

DAY 72

I Sought The Lord

"I sought the LORD, and He heard me, And delivered me from all my fears." Psalm 34:4

Notice how deliverance is preceded by, "I sought the LORD." Over and over in scripture, you will find the theme of seeking. For example:

1. "I love those who love me, And those who seek me diligently will find me." Proverbs 8:17
2. "And you will seek Me and find Me, when you search for Me with all your heart." Jeremiah 29:13
3. "For thus says the LORD to the house of Israel: "Seek Me   and live;" Amos 5:4

If you study any of the patriarchs, prophets, or disciples in the Bible, you will see how they sought the LORD in prayer. Prayer is seeking God, His Word, and His will. He who seeks finds and finding is the reward of seeking.

My prayer for you today is that you reap the reward of seeking after the LORD. "I called on the LORD in distress; The LORD answered me and set me in a broad place." Psalm 118:5

DAY 73

Return, O Backsliding Children

"Go and proclaim these words toward the north, and say: 'Return, backsliding Israel,' says the LORD; 'I will not cause My anger to fall on you. For I am merciful,' says the LORD; 'I will not remain angry forever. Only acknowledge your iniquity, That you have transgressed against the LORD your God, And have scattered your charms To alien deities under every green tree, And you have not obeyed My voice,' says the LORD. "Return, O backsliding children," says the LORD; "for I am married to you. I will take you, one from a city and two from a family, and I will bring you to Zion. And I will give you shepherds according to My heart, who will feed you with knowledge and understanding." Jeremiah 3:12-15

These pleas: "Return, O backsliding children" and "For I am married to you" have a great depth of feeling. This response is not from a cold, dispassionate God; this is the Lord full of mercy and compassion and who is pursuing His backsliding people. This plea, to me, is a picture of why revival is possible.

After the blessing of restoration, God promised the benefit of excellent and godly spiritual leadership, giving an instructive description of what leaders among God's people should be.

1. They should be given by God (I will give you), not by human ambition or presumed calling.
2. They give to the people of God (I will give you), and they show care and service unto them.

123

3. They should be shepherds caring for the flock of God.
4. They should be according to God's heart in the way they serve and lead God's people.
5. They should feed God's people with knowledge and understanding.

My prayer today is for revival and restoration. Please join me.

DAY 74

The Sovereignty of God

"The LORD has established His throne in heaven, And His kingdom rules over all." Psalm 103:19

My wife has a saying that she learned in Bible College, and it goes like this: "If HE who can doesn't, it must be better so." For those of us who define sovereignty as the fact that God is in control of and involved with everything in our life, we realize the truth of my wife's statement. It is God who opens and closes. For example in the book of Revelation reads: "And to the angel of the church in Philadelphia write, 'These things says He who is holy, He who is true, He who has the key of David, He who opens and no one shuts, and shuts and no one opens" (Revelation 3:7). This verse is also a prophetic fulfillment of the book of Isaiah that reads: "The key of the house of David I will lay on his shoulder; So he shall open, and no one shall shut; and he shall shut, and no one shall open." Isaiah 22:22

I want to encourage you today to trust God to open and close doors. Believe in His ultimate power and divine wisdom to guide you through life's journey. HE knows what is best because, as we read, "The LORD has established His throne in heaven, And His kingdom rules overall." That "all" means you!

My prayer for you today is: "Now He who searches the hearts knows what the mind of the Spirit is, because He makes intercession for the saints according to the will of God. And we know that all things work together for good to those who love God, to those who are the called according to His purpose." Romans 8:27-28

DAY 75

Don't belittle anything about Jesus

"Behold, the virgin shall be with child, and bear a Son, and they shall call His name Immanuel, which is translated, "God with us." Matthew 1:23

Matthew rightly understood that the supernatural conception of Jesus was prophesied in Isaiah 7:14. "Therefore the Lord Himself will give you a sign: Behold, the virgin shall conceive and bear a Son, and shall call His name Immanuel."

I heard someone say the other day: "the only thing that matters about Jesus is His death, burial, and resurrection." He went on to explain how we shouldn't be celebrating the birth of Jesus. My question is this: "Why wouldn't we celebrate everything about Jesus!?" There are several reasons to celebrate, but for me, this is most important: "For the testimony of Jesus is the spirit of prophecy." Revelation 19:10

One of the ways we can avoid unbiblical approaches to what we think is essential or not is by realizing prophecy is first and foremost a testimony about Jesus Christ. Therefore, when we study prophecy, we should search for the revelation of the beauty of Jesus. I believe that can include His birth.

My prayer for us today is that we celebrate everything about Jesus.

DAY 76

Overcome Evil With Good

"Never repay anyone evil for evil. Take thought for what is right and gracious and proper in the sight of everyone. If possible, as far as it depends on you, live at peace with everyone. Beloved, never avenge yourselves, but leave the way open for God's wrath [and His judicial righteousness]; for it is written [in Scripture], "VENGEANCE IS MINE, I WILL REPAY," says the Lord. "BUT IF YOUR ENEMY IS HUNGRY, FEED HIM; IF HE IS THIRSTY, GIVE HIM A DRINK; FOR BY DOING THIS YOU WILL HEAP BURNING COALS ON HIS HEAD." Do not be overcome and conquered by evil, but overcome evil with good." Romans 12:17-21 AMP

The Apostle Paul reminds us not to let an enemy's hostility produce hostility in us. In other words, it is not our job to unroot all of earth's evil. Instead, we are called to love our neighbors and enemies alike, knowing that God will deal with sin decisively when He returns. So, again, "Don't be overcome by his evil. Don't let another person's evil make you evil."

The one who trusts in God will not think it necessary to avenge themselves. They will leave the issue of vengeance to God and give place to wrath – giving no place to their own personal wrath, but rather a wide place to God's wrath. Overcome evil with good: With this mindset, we will do good to our enemies, looking for the most practical ways to bless them with hope. It is this mindset that enables us not to be overcome by evil but overcome evil with good.

My prayer for us today is that we remember: "For we are His workmanship, created in Christ Jesus for good works, which God prepared beforehand that we should walk in them." Ephesians 2:10

DAY 77

Staying Fit For The Kingdom of God

"And another also said, 'Lord, I will follow You, but let me first go and bid them farewell who are at my house.' But Jesus said to him, 'No one, having put his hand to the plow, and looking back, is fit for the kingdom of God.'" Luke 9:61-62

I woke up thinking about being "fit for the kingdom of God." The word "fit" in Greek has also been translated well placed or useful. In these verses, Jesus talks about a man who offered to follow Jesus after a delay. First, however, Jesus stressed to this man the commitment necessary to follow Him. Then, Jesus goes on to give an example of a farmer on a plow. The farmer was to keep the rows straight by focusing on an object in front of him (such as a tree). However, if the farmer started to plow and kept looking behind, he would never make straight rows and do a good job plowing. The Believer must have a similar determination as a farmer plowing a field; they must do it with all their strength and always looking forward. In following Jesus, we keep our eyes on Jesus and never take our eyes off Him.

The truth is, when you have a heart for the Kingdom of God, you will follow Jesus wholeheartedly and without delay. This determination is what makes you fit for the kingdom of God.

My prayer for us today is that we stay "fit" for the Kingdom of God.

DAY 78

Eternal Life

"My sheep hear My voice, and I know them, and they follow Me. And I give them eternal life, and they shall never perish; neither shall anyone snatch them out of My hand." John 10:27-28

Have you heard someone say, " I wish I could live forever!?" The good news is, you can! If you believe in Jesus, you will have an eternal home in heaven: "Jesus said to her, 'I am the resurrection and the life. He who believes in Me, though he may die, he shall live. And whoever lives and believes in Me shall never die. Do you believe this?'" John 11:25-26

My grandmother died at the young age of 42. I was not privileged to meet her since I was born after she had already passed away. I am thankful that I have learned that my grandmother was prepared for heaven because she had accepted Jesus in her life and now has an eternal home with God. This hope made her death bearable to my mother, who lost her mom at 14. My grandmother is gone from her earthly life, but we will be reunited with her in God's kingdom one day. I will see my grandmother again: "For we know that if our earthly house, this tent, is destroyed, we have a building from God, a house not made with hands, eternal in the heavens." 2 Corinthians 5:1

If you know someone who does not know Jesus, please introduce them to Jesus. We can't force a person to know Jesus, but we can give them the opportunity. The choice will then be up to them: "that whoever believes in Him should not perish but have eternal life. For God so loved the world that He gave His only begotten Son, that whoever believes in Him should not perish but have everlasting life." John 3:15-16

My prayer for you today is that you receive and share the promise of eternal life: "And this is the promise that He has promised us—eternal life." 1 John 2:25

DAY 79

Salvation

"That if you confess with your mouth the Lord Jesus and believe in your heart that God has raised Him from the dead, you will be saved. For with the heart one believes unto righteousness, and with the mouth confession is made unto salvation." Romans 10:9-10

The word salvation means "deliverance." It can mean deliverance from fear, enemies, sin, sickness, death, our fleshly bodies, even from eternal judgment. Those who confess that "salvation is of the Lord" acknowledge that we human beings cannot save ourselves. The enemies of our souls are too strong, and within ourselves, we are too weak. Therefore we are entirely dependent on God.

The name Yeshua (Jesus) appropriately means "the salvation of God," and this promise has been given to, "Whoever calls on the name of the LORD shall be saved" (Acts 2:21). Thus, in the scriptures, he is referred to as the rock of our salvation, to whom we "shout joyfully" (Psalm 95:1).
Jesus is also referred to as the captain of our salvation, who was made "perfect through suffering" (Hebrews 2:10), and the author of eternal salvation "to all who obey Him" (Hebrews 5:9).

My prayer for us today is that we believe in who He is and to come into alignment with His Word and will. So let the church say AMEN!

133

DAY 80

I Will Look On It To Remember

"And I will remember My covenant which is between Me and you and every living creature of all flesh; the waters shall never again become a flood to destroy all flesh. The rainbow shall be in the cloud, and I will look on it to remember the everlasting covenant between God and every living creature of all flesh that is on the earth." Genesis 9:15-16

I am not sure what comes to mind when you see a rainbow, but I know what should come to mind. Besides its beauty in the sky, we need to remember the promise that God has made. This promise is an everlasting covenant between He and every living creature of all flesh on the earth. The other mentions of a rainbow in the Bible are in the context of God's enthroned glory (Ezekiel 1:28; Revelation 4:3 and 10:1). It is beautiful to see God, in His glory, positioning one close to Himself as a reminder of His promise to humanity.

A scientist once shared with me that a rainbow can be seen by someone in the world every day. This insight is a beautiful picture of God looking upon the remembrance of HIS covenant promises every day.

My prayer for you today is that every time you see a rainbow, you will remember every one of God's promises and also His GREAT faithfulness.

DAY 81

Wisdom From God

"Who is wise and understanding among you? Let him show by good conduct that his works are done in the meekness of wisdom. But if you have bitter envy and self-seeking in your hearts, do not boast and lie against the truth. This wisdom does not descend from above, but is earthly, sensual, demonic. For where envy and self-seeking exist, confusion and every evil thing are there. But the wisdom that is from above is first pure, then peaceable, gentle, willing to yield, full of mercy and good fruits, without partiality and without hypocrisy. Now the fruit of righteousness is sown in peace by those who make peace." James 3:13-18

James contrasts the peaceful wisdom, which is "from above," with the contentious wisdom, which is from the devil. From "above" is a Jewish way of saying, "from God." Wisdom is not mere head knowledge. Real wisdom and understanding will show in our lives by our good conduct. In other words, if a person considers himself to be wise or understanding, it is fair to expect that this inner quality would show itself in regular life. Here James told us how to judge if a person is wise and understanding.

In this statement, "But the wisdom that is from above," James is defining the meekness of wisdom. First pure, then peaceable, gentle, willing to yield, full of mercy and good fruits, without partiality and without hypocrisy: The character of this wisdom is terrific. It is full of love and a giving heart, consistent with the holiness of God. God's wisdom has fruit.

135

My prayer for us today is that we would receive wisdom from God.

DAY 82

The Power of the Word of God

"For the word of God is alive and active. Sharper than any double-edged sword, it penetrates even to dividing soul and spirit, joints and marrow; it judges the thoughts and attitudes of the heart." Hebrews 4:12 NIV

God's Word diagnoses the condition of the man with a surgeon's precision. It lays open our hearts and discerns our spiritual health.

The Word of God is Powerful (translated active in the KJV) reminds us that something may be alive yet dormant. But God's Word is both living and powerful, in the sense of being active.

The Bible isn't a collection of old stories and myths. It has inherent life and power. The preacher doesn't make the Bible come alive. The Bible is purposeful and gives life to the preacher and anyone else who will receive it with faith.

Be encouraged, God's Word reaches us with surprising precision, and the Holy Spirit empowers the ministry of the Word to work sincerely in our hearts.

My prayer today is Ephesians 6-17 "And take the helmet of salvation, and the sword of the Spirit, which is the word of God."

DAY 83

That I May Know You

"Now therefore, I pray, if I have found grace in Your sight, show me now Your way, that I may know You and that I may find grace in Your sight. And consider that this nation is Your people. And He said, 'My Presence will go with you, and I will give you rest.'" Exodus 33:13-14

A strong theme in this section is to know. In some form, the word is used repeatedly in these verses. God knew Israel and Moses in the sense of relationship, and Moses wanted to know God's "way," the God-inspired path that he should follow. He asked to know God's way, but his real passion was to know God's nature. Moses requested this so that ultimately he could experience even more or the grace of God. The word translated "grace" is *chen*, and it comes from the root word "*chanan*" which means to stoop down in order to help one who is inferior. Whenever God pours out grace, in a sense, He "stoops down" from His level of holiness and perfection to help sinful and imperfect humanity simply because He loves us.

It is beautiful to read how Moses continued to press God for affirmation of the promise. This plea shows how boldly he sought after God for the sake of his relationship with God and the nation's benefit. My Presence will go with you is literally "My Face will go with you." This statement helps us understand what it means when it says Moses met with God face to face (Exodus 32:11). It has the sense of being "in the immediate presence of God."

My prayer for us today is: "that the God of our Lord Jesus Christ, the Father of glory, may give to you the spirit of wisdom and revelation in the knowledge of Him, the eyes of your understanding being enlightened; that you may know what is the hope of His calling, what are the riches of the glory of His inheritance in the saints, and what is the exceeding greatness of His power toward us who believe, according to the working of His mighty power" Ephesians 1:17-19

DAY 84

Anxious

"Be anxious for nothing, but in everything by prayer and supplication, with thanksgiving, let your requests be made known to God; and the peace of God, which surpasses all understanding, will guard your hearts and minds through Christ Jesus." Philippians 4:6-7

The command to "be anxious for nothing." is very difficult, especially at certain seasons of our lives. But, the truth is, anxiety can cripple someone's life. It can bring someone into deep depression or despair.

Strong's Definitions: μεριμνάω merimnáō; to be anxious about:—(be, have) care(-ful), take thought, to be worried.

The answers to anxiety are experienced in these words: But in everything by prayer and supplication: Paul wrote that everything is the proper subject of prayer. In other words, there are no areas of our lives that are not a concern to God.

In Luke, we read the story of Mary and Martha: "And Jesus answered and said to her, "Martha, Martha, you are worried and troubled about many things." (Luke 10:41). The word "worried" is the same Greek word found in Philippians 4:6. Jesus also answers how we are anxious for nothing. Jesus said: Mary has chosen the good part, which will not be taken away from her: Mary's good part was her simple devotion to Jesus, loving Him by listening to His word. This devotion was Mary's chosen focus.

We really can be anxious for nothing, pray about everything, and be thankful for God's promises.

My prayer for us today is: "pray without ceasing, in everything give thanks; for this is the will of God in Christ Jesus for you. 1 Thessalonians 5:17-18

DAY 85

My Hands

"I spread out my hands to You; My soul longs for You like a thirsty land. Selah" Psalm 143:6

I don't believe there is a set or specific physical position for our prayers to be heard. In other words, you can be walking, standing, sitting, kneeling, or prostrate on the floor. Or you can have your head and hands lifted. None of these positions are "sacred keys" that ensure the answer we seek will come. However, that being said, we still need to understand that the lifting of hands in worship is highly symbolic and, at times, even prophetic. It is a prayer method found over and over in the Word of God. For example:

"Let us lift our hearts and hands To God in heaven." Lamentations 3:41

"My hands also I will lift up to Your commandments, Which I love, And I will meditate on Your statutes." Psalm 119:48

"I desire therefore that the men pray everywhere, lifting up holy hands, without wrath and doubting;" 1 Timothy 2:8

Based on the scriptures just quoted, when we lift our hands in prayer and praise, we are:

1. Lifting our hearts up to God

2. Expressing love for, and submission to, His commandments

3. Surrendering to God and no longer harboring anger, bitterness, or unforgiveness toward God or people.

My prayer for us today: "Let my prayer be set before You as incense, The lifting up of my hands as the evening sacrifice." Psalm 141:2

DAY 86

Wisdom & Knowledge

"Now give me wisdom and knowledge, that I may go out and come in before this people; for who can judge this great people of Yours?" 2 Chronicles 1:10

God gave an immediate response to Solomon's prayer, prophesying that he would receive more than what he asked for, granting him "riches, and wealth and honor" (2 Chronicles 1:12). Shortly after receiving his gifts, Solomon demonstrated great wisdom in dealing with two women fighting over who was the rightful mother of a living child (1 Kings 3:16-28). When he resolved the problematic issue with spiritual discernment, "all Israel heard of the judgment which the king had rendered; and they feared the king, for they saw that the wisdom of God was in him to administer justice" (1 Kings 3:28).

My question for us today is, where are we seeking wisdom and knowledge? A good indicator is where we spend our time, study, and resources.

My prayer for us today is: "My son, if you receive my words, And treasure my commands within you, So that you incline your ear to wisdom, And apply your heart to understanding; Yes, if you cry out for discernment, And lift up your voice for understanding, If you seek her as silver, And search for her as for hidden treasures; Then you will understand the fear of the LORD, And find the knowledge of God. For the LORD gives wisdom; From His mouth come knowledge and understanding; He stores up sound wisdom for the upright; He is a shield to those who walk uprightly;" Proverbs 2:1-7

DAY 87

Shalom, Shalom

"You will keep him in perfect peace, Whose mind is stayed on You, Because he trusts in You." Isaiah 26:3

God wants us to know HIS peace amid judgment. Not just any peace, but the very peace that comes from hearing HIS voice. Perfect peace! HE promises that we can have perfect peace and even be kept in a place of perfect peace.

In Hebrew, the term perfect peace is shalom shalom. This emphasis reveals how in Hebrew, repetition communicates intensity. It isn't just shalom; it is shalom shalom, perfect peace.

To be kept in this perfect peace is a matter of our minds. We are to love the LORD our God with all of our minds (Matthew 22:37). We are transformed by the renewing of our minds (Romans 12:2). We can have the mind of Christ (1 Corinthians 2:16, Philippians 2:5). We are not to set our mind on earthly things (Philippians 3:19), but to set our mind on things above (Colossians 3:2). The Believer's life is not a thoughtless life of just doing or experiencing, but it is also about thinking, and where we set our minds is essential in our walk before the LORD.

To be kept in this perfect peace, our mind must stay on the LORD. Proverbs 3:5 expresses this same idea: Trust in the LORD with all your heart, and lean not on your own understanding. The word for lean in Proverbs 3:5 comes from the same root as the word stayed in Isaiah 26:3. When we trust in the LORD, we do not lean on our own understanding. To lean on the LORD is to trust Him. To be sustained by the LORD is to trust Him. To be established by the LORD is to trust Him. To be upheld by the LORD is to trust Him.

My prayer for us today is that we experience HIS Shalom Shalom.

DAY 88

His Good Pleasure

"For it is God who works in you both to will and to do for His good pleasure. Do all things without complaining and disputing, that you may become blameless and harmless, children of God without fault in the midst of a crooked and perverse generation, among whom you shine as lights in the world, holding fast the word of life, so that I may rejoice in the day of Christ that I have not run in vain or labored in vain." Philippians 2:13-16

How are you different from those around you? Take a look at your speech. Those without God tend to be careless with their speech. It is common for the unrepentant to speak lies, quarrel, gossip, repeat confidence, state the obvious, talk negative, complain, boast, curse, find fault. How are you any different from those who have not been made sons and daughters of God the Father through belief in His Son's death and resurrection?

What about your actions? The truth is, those who have not yet acknowledged their guilt and need for help tend to act out in a hurtful and harmful way. Their actions reveal their thoughts and heart. Stealing, fighting, killing, abusive, drunkards, sexually active outside of marriage, unfaithful, arrogant, rude, selfish are some of these actions without the power of God that brings change. So, looking at your actions, do you represent Jesus so that others would know there is something different about you, that you possess traits that they would aspire to obtain?

The compromised life affects me and the Body of Christ as well as the unrepentant lives around us. And as a direct result, lives lost, broken, addicted, sick, and demon-possessed have no idea that there is SOMEONE who can radically change their lives and very existence.

We are the salt(preservation) and light(the way) to the countless souls around us. Are you salty? Are you shinning? How will they ever know if our lives don't exhibit hope for a change? The world around us is dependent upon us to be like Jesus. They don't even know it yet. They are clueless to understand that we possess what they are groping in the dark for in their lives.

My prayer for us today is that we are brought into His likeness because it's that likeness that has the power to effect change in the lives of those around us.

DAY 89

Wait on the LORD

"I would have lost heart, unless I had believed that I would see the goodness of the LORD In the land of the living. Wait on the LORD; Be of good courage, And He shall strengthen your heart; Wait, I say, on the LORD!" Psalm 27:13-14

When you and I are in a crisis or a difficult season of life, it can be challenging to wait on the LORD for an answer. Waiting for God is not always easy. Sometimes it can seem like God isn't answering or doesn't understand the urgency of the hour. However, that kind of thinking can lead to the feeling that God is not in control or that He is unjust. Truthfully, this type of attack in our minds can be a subtle attempt of the devil to keep you and me from seeking God for courage and strength. Therefore, we must understand that God is worth waiting for no matter the difficulty. "The LORD is my portion, says my soul; therefore I hope in Him! The LORD is good to those who wait for Him, To the soul who seeks Him. It is good that one should hope and wait quietly For the salvation of the LORD." Lam. 3:24-26

We need to be reminded that God often uses waiting on HIM to refresh, renew, and strengthen our hearts. So let us make good use of seasons of waiting on HIM by discovering how God may be working more of HIS character in and through us.

My prayer for us today is that we learn to wait upon the LORD: "But those who wait on the LORD Shall renew their

150

strength; They shall mount up with wings like eagles, They shall run and not be weary, They shall walk and not faint."

DAY 90

You Are

"You also, as living stones, are being built up a spiritual house, a holy priesthood, to offer up spiritual sacrifices acceptable to God through Jesus Christ....But you are a chosen generation, a royal priesthood, a holy nation, His own special people, that you may proclaim the praises of Him who called you out of darkness into His marvelous light;" 1 Peter 2:5, 9

Under the new covenant, all believers are priests. They do not need any mediator except their great High Priest, Jesus. In other words, there is no longer an elite priesthood with claims of special access to God or special privileges in worship or fellowship with God. Instead, the believer is their own priest before God.

His own special people: We are "special" because we belong to God. A museum may be filled with ordinary things: clothes, canes, shoes, and so forth, but they may be significant because they once belonged to someone famous. God takes ordinary people, and because He works in and through them, they are "special."

It is essential to mention that the purpose of this special calling is not to grow proud but to proclaim the praises of Him who has done such great things for us.

My prayer for us today is, knowing who we are, that we may proclaim the praises of Him who called us out of darkness into His marvelous light.

DAY 91

The Accusers

"When Jesus had raised Himself up and saw no one but the woman, He said to her, 'Woman, where are those accusers of yours? Has no one condemned you?'" John 8:10

Accusations can be very painful and damaging. They are tools of the enemy of our soul to bring us into guilt, shame, and ultimately bondage.

In John 8, a woman is brought to Jesus, caught in the act of adultery. The religious leaders brought this woman to Jesus in shame-filled, humiliating circumstances. They did this as Jesus publicly taught in the temple courts. They wanted to accuse and condemn the woman publicly so that they could ultimately expose Jesus.

The religious leaders – condemning men as they were – used this woman as a weapon against Jesus. First, they presented her as a sinner before Jesus but ignored their own sin in the matter. Then, finally, the accusers left as Jesus was bowed down to the ground, writing in the dirt.

The accusations from our enemies mean nothing against us because Jesus has already paid the penalty our sins deserved. We may be even worse than Satan's accusations, but we are still made righteous by the work of Jesus on the cross (Ephesians 1:7, Colossians 1:14, and Hebrews 9:14). The blood, our testimony, and humility before God overcome Satan's accusations. "And they overcame him by the blood of the Lamb and by the word of their testimony, and they did not love their lives to the death." Revelation 12:11

Be blessed with hope today: "Then I heard a loud voice saying in heaven, 'Now salvation, and strength, and the kingdom of our God, and the power of His Christ have come, for the accuser of our brethren, who accused them before our God day and night, has been cast down.'" Revelation 12:10

DAY 92

The Favor From The LORD

"He who finds a wife finds a good thing, And obtains favor from the LORD." Proverbs 18:22

It's important to note where the "favor" comes from in our lives. I rejoice in the favor that comes "from the LORD."

This verse also reminds me that marriage is blessed by God when we acknowledge HIM and do marriage HIS way. Today's emphasis on individual freedom is misguided. Strong individuals are essential, but so are united solid marriages. God created marriage for our enjoyment, and He pronounced it good and favorable. Marriage is a gift from God that, when acknowledged, brings blessing upon blessing.

I've adapted this principle for our marriage: When she wins, I win, and when she loses, I lose. We shouldn't compete against each other because we are one. The "Favor" comes from knowing that marriage is God's gift of oneness. "Therefore a man shall leave his father and mother and be joined to his wife, and they shall become one flesh." Genesis 2:24

I leave you with one final passage. It is the scripture that I read yearly: "Drink water from your own cistern and running water from your own well. Should your fountains be dispersed abroad, Streams of water in the streets? Let them be only your own, And not for strangers with you. Let your fountain be blessed, And rejoice with the wife of your youth. As a loving deer and a graceful doe, Let her breasts satisfy

156

you at all times; And always be enraptured with her love."
Proverbs 5:15-19

My prayer for us today is that we would be able to recognize
"favor from the LORD" and rejoice in it.

DAY 93

Never Leave You

"Let your conduct be without covetousness; be content with such things as you have. For He Himself has said, "I will never leave you nor forsake you." Hebrews 13:5

Real contentment and joy come from trust in God to meet our needs and to be our security. Yet, strangely we are often more likely to put safety and find contentment in things far less reliable and secure than God Himself.

Being alone is hard. Often, we as humans find ourselves discontent when we are alone. The truth is, we were created for community, not confinement. However, we can be grateful today that no matter how alone we may feel, the LORD will never leave or forsake us. We can also be grateful for the technology that has helped us stay in touch with each other. Today, we can be reminded that this season of social distancing and isolation will not last forever. God has been faithful to give us the strength to endure this difficult season and deepen our connection with Our Heavenly Father and His people.

My prayer for us today is that God would empower us with an extra dose of HIS love, peace, hope, and joy because we need it.

DAY 94

His Government

"For unto us a Child is born, Unto us a Son is given; And the government will be upon His shoulder. And His name will be called Wonderful, Counselor, Mighty God, Everlasting Father, Prince of Peace. Of the increase of His government and peace there will be no end, Upon the throne of David and over His kingdom, To order it and establish it with judgment and justice From that time forward, even forever. The zeal of the LORD of hosts will perform this." Isaiah 9:6-7

Did you read those beautiful words?: "His government and peace there will be no end."

Peter Marshall, the Chaplain of the U.S. Senate (1947-1949), once issued a call for Americans to honor God. He said: "The choice before us is plain: Christ or chaos, conviction or compromise, discipline or disintegration. I am rather tired of hearing about our rights and privilege as American citizens. The time has come - it is now - when we ought to hear about the duties and responsibilities of our citizenship. America's future depends upon her accepting and demonstrating God's government."

His government shows its workings in beautiful ways. Whenever I see someone who miraculously leaves a life of drugs or alcohol and is restored to his family and work, I can see that God now governs him. Whenever I see loving Christians gently caring for orphans and those rejected by family, I know I am watching people governed by God.

159

Whenever I see people eagerly learning the Bible and joyously praising, I know who the governor is. Whenever I see people give up lucrative careers to go and share the Good News of Jesus, I know God governs them. When I see pastors carefully teach and lead the flock God has given them, I know they are getting signals from the great King.

The truth is, some leaders of our day use their power to build their empires. However, Jesus used His power to wash the disciple's feet and make them clean. Then He told them to go and do likewise.

DAY 95

Your First Love

"I know your works, your labor, your patience, and that you cannot bear those who are evil. And you have tested those who say they are apostles and are not, and have found them liars; and you have persevered and have patience, and have labored for My name's sake and have not become weary. Nevertheless I have this against you, that you have left your first love. Remember therefore from where you have fallen; repent and do the first works, or else I will come to you quickly and remove your lampstand from its place—unless you repent." Revelation 2:2-5

Despite all the good in the Ephesian church, there is something seriously wrong. Without love, all in vain. No wonder Jesus said, "Nevertheless, I have this against you."

It is interesting to note that they had left – not lost – their first love. They once had a love that they don't have anymore. The distinction between leaving and losing is essential. Something can be lost by accident, but leaving is usually a deliberate act, though it may not happen suddenly. When we lose something, we don't know where to find it; but when we leave something, we know where to find it.

What love did they leave? As Believers, we are instructed to love God and to love one another. Did they leave their love for God? Did they leave their love for one another? Probably both are in mind because the two loves go together. You can't say you love God and not love His family, and you can't love

His family without loving Him first. Could it also mean that their message had changed from what God had given them (the word of God) to becoming an echo of society? What our hearts become filled with will eventually come out of our mouths.

My prayer for us today is that these words would be in our hearts: "I will delight myself in Your statutes; I will not forget Your word." Psalm 119:16

DAY 96

O LORD of Host

*"O LORD of hosts, God of Israel, the One who dwells
between the cherubim, You are God, You alone, of all the
kingdoms of the earth. You have made heaven and earth."*
Isaiah 37:16

To appreciate Hezekiah's prayer, we must understand the
context. In 721 BC, the Assyrian army under Sennacherib
invaded and destroyed the northern kingdom of Israel.
Around that time, the Jews of the southern kingdom began
paying tribute to Sennacherib. But at a certain point,
Hezekiah refused to continue this practice, and Sennacherib
marched on Jerusalem with a massive army. His
representative, Rabshakeh, reviled them for their rebellion
and ridiculed them for their faith in God. Thus, for example,
we read: "Beware lest Hezekiah persuaded you, saying, 'The
LORD will deliver us.' Has any one of the gods of the nations
delivered its land from the hand of the king of
Assyria?" (Isaiah 36:18). However, Hezekiah had received a
prophecy from Isaiah three years prior that foretold the
destruction of the Assyrian army (Isaiah 10:24, 27).

So when Hezekiah received a letter from Sennacherib filled
with taunts, insults, and threats, he took it before the Lord
(Isaiah 37:14-23). He prayed, and God responded
supernaturally to Hezekiah's prayer by sending an angel of
the LORD into the camp of the Assyrians. In one night's time,
185,000 of them were slaughtered by this invisible heavenly

163

being. Miraculously the Israelites were spared without an arrow being shot or a spear being thrown.

My prayer for us today is that God would save us, defend us, deliver us, rescue us, and preserve us. May we see His glory!

DAY 97

Salvation

"That if you confess with your mouth the Lord Jesus and believe in your heart that God has raised Him from the dead, you will be saved. For with the heart one believes unto righteousness, and with the mouth confession is made unto salvation." Romans 10:9-10

The word salvation means "deliverance." It can mean deliverance from fear, enemies, sin, sickness, death, our fleshly bodies, even from eternal judgment. Those who confess that "salvation is of the Lord" acknowledge that we human beings cannot save ourselves. The enemies of our souls are too strong, and within ourselves, we are too weak. Therefore we are entirely dependent on God.

The name Yeshua (Jesus) appropriately means "the salvation of God," and this promise has been given to those who call upon Him: "Whoever calls on the name of the LORD shall be saved" (Acts 2:21). We also read in the scriptures how Jesus is: The rock of our salvation, to whom we "shout joyfully" (Psalm 95:1). The captain of our salvation, who was made "perfect through suffering" (Hebrews 2:10). The author of eternal salvation "to all who obey Him" (Hebrews 5:9).

My prayer for us today is that we believe in who He is. So let the church say AMEN!

DAY 98

The Significance of Prophecy

"And I fell at his feet to worship him. But he said to me, 'See that you do not do that! I am your fellow servant, and of your brethren who have the testimony of Jesus. Worship God! For the testimony of Jesus is the spirit of prophecy.'" Revelation 19:10

In the book of Revelation, an angel gave John the interpretive key to Bible prophecy. Prophecy exists to provide a witness of who Jesus Christ is. Most certainly, HE alone is the ultimate focus of prophecy.

For example:
1. Jesus Christ is the central Person of history.
2. Jesus Christ is at the very center of God's plan to redeem man. In other words, HE is God's answer to the wickedness and bondage found in the heart of man.
3. Jesus Christ is the answer to the crisis of this age - past, present, and future. When we lift HIM to HIS rightful place, the evil in this age will be judged, and the truth will prevail.

Once again, the true spirit of prophecy always shows itself in bearing witness to Jesus. Therefore, teaching or preaching on prophecy that takes our minds and hearts away from JESUS is not communicated correctly.

My prayer for us today is that we understand that prophecy, at its very heart, is designed to unfold the beauty and loveliness of our Lord and Savior, Jesus Christ.

DAY 99

Resisting The Truth

"Now as Jannes and Jambres resisted Moses, so do these also resist the truth: men of corrupt minds, disapproved concerning the faith; but they will progress no further, for their folly will be manifest to all, as theirs also was." 2 Timothy 3:8-9

Though they were not named in the Exodus account, these two men are most likely the Egyptian magicians who opposed Moses before Pharaoh (Exodus 7:8-13, 7:19-23, 8:5-7, and 8:16-19). Jannes and Jambres were able to work miracles by the power of darkness and not the power of God. For example, when Moses cast down his rod, and it turned into a serpent, Jannes and Jambres could do the same. When he turned water into blood, they could do the same. When Moses brought forth a plague of frogs, Jannes and Jambres could do the same. Eventually, however, they could not match the God of Moses, miracle-for-miracle. The occultic powers of Jannes and Jambres ultimately were shown to be inferior to God's power.

The ability to do miracles by the power of darkness and the willingness to receive them as authentic will characterize the end times (Revelation 13:13-15 and 2 Thessalonians 2:9). The truth is, we need to guard ourselves against being amazed by any spiritual power because that power may have a demonic source instead of a Godly one. And even if a psychic or new age power seems to feel right, we must not be seduced by it because demonic forces can come masquerading as

168

angels of light (2 Corinthians 11:15). The resistance of truth by Jannes and Jambres was shown by their ability to cooperate with demonic powers to do miracles. In the last days, men will also resist the truth of God's Word. This truth can even sound like hate to those who hate the scriptures. However, eventually, their folly will be exposed to all.

My prayer for us today is that we would be able to recognize the folly of those who resist the truth.

DAY 100

Friend of the Bridegroom

"He who has the bride is the bridegroom; but the friend of the bridegroom, who stands and hears him, rejoices greatly because of the bridegroom's voice. Therefore this joy of mine is fulfilled. He must increase, but I must decrease." John 3:29-30

John explained to his followers that he was like the best man at a wedding; he wasn't the Bridegroom. In other words, he isn't to be the focus of attention but to supervise the bringing of two people together.

In the Jewish wedding customs of that day, the friend of the Bridegroom arranged many of the wedding details and brought the bride to the groom. Nevertheless, the friend of the Bridegroom was never the focus of attention and wanted it that way. Simply put, John wanted his followers to know that all these arrangements fulfilled his joy.

One might say that John the Baptist lost his congregation – and he was happy about it! John was happy because he lost his followers to Jesus, the true Bridegroom.

My prayer for us today is that we too would be a true friend of the Bride Groom who says, "He must increase, but I must decrease." John 3:30

DAY 101

Trust In HIS Name

"Trust in the LORD forever, For in YAH, the LORD, is everlasting strength." Isaiah 26:4

In the scripture above, the form of God's name is "YAH" (like the last syllable of the worship word "Hallelujah," which means "praise to YAH." Theologians have said that God's name is most likely Yahweh or Yahovah. Drawn from the Hebrew letters YHWH and traditionally called the Tetragrammaton, it was initially written in the Hebrew language with only consonants, no vowels. In most English Bibles, YHWH is rendered "Lord" (Thousands of times). But the word Lord means "Master," so it is an insufficient rendering.

Unfortunately, at some point in the history of Israel, because of numerous times of destruction, dispersion, and enslavement, and because of a holy concern of breaking the third commandment, the correct pronunciation of YHWH was lost. However, this I believe is the beautiful revelation, Yahovah or Yahweh of the Old Testament is the Jesus (or more perfectly in the Hebrew, Yeshua) of the New Testament - because He always has been and always will be "the image of the invisible God" (Colossians 1:15). Therefore, Yeshua, which means "the salvation of God," is described as the name above every name.

My prayer for us today is that we trust in HIS NAME: "Therefore God also has highly exalted Him and given Him

171

the name which is above every name, that at the name of Jesus every knee should bow, of those in heaven, and of those on earth, and of those under the earth, and that every tongue should confess that Jesus Christ is Lord, to the glory of God the Father. Philippians 2:9-11

DAY 102

Everlasting Remembrance

"Surely he will never be shaken; The righteous will be in everlasting remembrance. He will not be afraid of evil tidings; His heart is steadfast, trusting in the LORD." Psalm 112:6-7

It is important to note that God is never challenged with His memory. On the contrary, he has total recall when he desires. And powerful, supernatural things happen when God brings His people to remembrance, such as: "Now it happened in the process of time that the king of Egypt died. Then the children of Israel groaned because of the bondage, and they cried out; and their cry came up to God because of the bondage. So God heard they're groaning, and God remembered His covenant with Abraham, with Isaac, and with Jacob" (Exodus 2:23-24). From that point forward, extraordinary and supernatural intervention took place to get God's people to the Promised Land.

This reassuring truth is also revealed in Hebrews 6:10, "For God is not unjust to forget your work and labor of love which you have shown toward His name." So if God failed to remember His covenant with you and your faithfulness toward Him, He would consider it an unjust or unrighteous thing. Faithfulness is who God is, and to remember is a part of His ethical and moral character.

My prayer for us today is that we would take comfort knowing, "The righteous will be in everlasting remembrance" (See Romans 5:18-19 on how we are made righteous).

DAY 103

Have Not Seen and Yet Believe

"And Thomas answered and said to Him, 'My Lord and my God!' Then Jesus told him [Thomas], 'Because you have seen Me, you have believed; blessed are those who have not seen and yet have believed.'" John 20:28-29

None of us living today has ever seen, in person, George Washington. We can read about him, hear stories passed down about him, and even view places he once occupied. However, we have never seen him, and if seeing is always believing, George Washington in a fairytale.

Thomas is often known as Doubting Thomas. Thomas refused to believe the testimony of many witnesses and reliable sources. Instead, he made an extreme demand for evidence, evidence of not only sight but of touch, and to repeatedly touch the multiple wounds of Jesus. Thomas steadfastly refused to believe unless he could see for himself. Perhaps Thomas had abandoned hope; – the strong evidence of his senses had finally convinced him that the pierced side, the wounded hands, and the cruel death made it impossible for him to believe.

Following His resurrection, while appearing to Thomas, Jesus spoke of a future group who were to one day believe in Him (John 20:29). Those of us who are a part of that group do not have to see Jesus with our physical eyes to believe. That is the wondrous blessing of faith. Seeing may not be believing, but believing is seeing! "Whom having not seen you love.

175

Though now you do not see Him, yet believing, you rejoice with joy inexpressible and full of glory, receiving the end of your faith—the salvation of your souls." 1 Peter 1:8-9

Today, I pray that we rejoice with joy unspeakable as we walk by faith with the One who is crowned with glory and honor! "But we do see Him who was made for a little while lower than the angels, namely, Jesus, because of the suffering of death crowned with glory and honor" (Hebrews 2:9a).

DAY 104

The Call To Worship

"Let us come before His presence with thanksgiving; Let us shout joyfully to Him with psalms." Psalm 95:2

This 95th psalm is a call to worship. This invitation is a call to worship the LORD with purpose. It describes "how" and "why" God is to be praised. For example:

OH Come - Let Us
1. LET US Sing to the LORD (v. 1).
2. LET US shout joyfully to the rock of our salvation (v. 1).
3. LET US come before HIS presence with thanksgiving (v. 2).
4. LET US shout joyfully to Him with psalms (v. 2).
5. LET US worship and bow down (v. 6).
6. LET US kneel before the LORD our Maker (v. 6).

Prayer is heard when knees cannot bend, but it seems that a humble and reverent heart should show its awe by prostrating the body and bending the knee when it is possible. Posture is not everything, yet is it something.

My prayer for us today is that we recognize our call to worship. "Oh come, let us worship and bow down; Let us kneel before the LORD our Maker." Psalm 95:6

DAY 105

Wait On The LORD

"He gives power to the weak, And to those who have no might He increases strength. Even the youths shall faint and be weary, And the young men shall utterly fall, But those who wait on the LORD Shall renew their strength; They shall mount up with wings like eagles, They shall run and not be weary, They shall walk and not faint." Isaiah 40:29-31

Waiting can seem complicated, frustrating, and even depressing when you don't feel like you are making any progress. The key to waiting is knowing "who" you're ultimately waiting for in prayer. We wait on the LORD with great anticipation because HE is a promise keeper.

Weak in Isaiah 40:29 and faint in Isaiah 40:30 are the same Hebrew word, which means "failure through loss of inherent strength." Weary in Isaiah 40:30 is a different word, which implies exhaustion because of the hardness of life. If we are weak for either reason, God is here to give us strength - if we will wait on Him! Truth be known, it is the LORD who has everything we need. When "HE" becomes the source of our waiting, we come into the following:

1. HE Renews us
2. HE Strengthens us
3. HE Gives Vision to us
4. HE Gives Endurance to us
5. HE Keeps us Alive

178

My prayer for us today is that we experienced the joy of waiting. "Wait on the LORD; Be of good courage, And He shall strengthen your heart; Wait, I say, on the LORD!" Psalm 27:14

DAY 106

The Power of the Cross

"For the message of the cross is foolishness to those who are perishing, but to us who are being saved it is the power of God." 1 Corinthians 1:18

Have you ever met a person who thought your belief in Jesus was foolish? Well, instead of getting upset or offended, it should remind you of the truth of God's Word: "For the message of the cross is foolishness to those who are perishing."

The message of the cross may sound kind of noble and religious to our twenty-first-century views. But in the first century, saying "message of the cross" was about the same as saying the message of the electric chair – except worse! What message does a cruel, humiliating, unrelenting instrument of death have? However, though it is a strange message, and regarded as foolish by the perishing, to those who trust in it and are being saved, this message of the cross becomes to us the actual power of God.

The verb tenses of are perishing and are being saved are significant. They both describe a work in progress. Each of us is moving in one of those two directions. This motivation is why we proclaim the gospel (good news) that says: "For God so loved the world that He gave His only begotten Son, that whoever believes in Him should not perish but have everlasting life. For God did not send His Son into the world

180

to condemn the world, but that the world through Him might be saved." John 3:16-17

My prayer for us today is that the message of the cross would remind us of HIS power.

DAY 107

Take Careful Attention

"But take careful heed to do the commandment and the law which Moses the servant of the LORD commanded you, to love the LORD your God, to walk in all His ways, to keep His commandments, to hold fast to Him, and to serve Him with all your heart and with all your soul." Joshua 22:5

When the Lord's people entered the Promised Land in Joshua's day, the Lord told them how they should live. These commands are still safeguards today. It is healthy for our souls if we hold fast to these words. It is beneficial to our lives if we please and serve the LORD with all of our hearts.

Let's take a closer look at the order of our responses:
To heed His commandments, we must take care to hear God.

1. Love the LORD your God
2. Walk-in all His ways
3. Keep His commandments
4. Hold fast to Him
5. Serve Him with all your heart and all your soul

We have to "take care" because many temptations and deceptive practices would try to pull us away.

My prayer for us today is that we keep His commandments, hold fast to Him and serve Him with all of our heart and soul.

DAY 108

Who is wise and understanding?

"Who is wise and understanding among you? Let him show by good conduct that his works are done in the meekness of wisdom. But if you have bitter envy and self-seeking in your hearts, do not boast and lie against the truth. This wisdom does not descend from above, but is earthly, sensual, demonic. For where envy and self-seeking exist, confusion and every evil thing are there. But the wisdom that is from above is first pure, then peaceable, gentle, willing to yield, full of mercy and good fruits, without partiality and without hypocrisy. Now the fruit of righteousness is sown in peace by those who make peace." James 3:13-18

The word *sophos* ('wise') was the technical term among the Jews for the teacher, the scribe, or the rabbi. It appears that James is still speaking to those who would be teachers (3:1); here, it is not what they say that he is concerned with, but rather how they live.

The passage of scripture is helping us understand that wisdom is not mere head knowledge. Real wisdom and understanding will show in our lives by our good conduct. True wisdom is also evident in humility and good behavior. Those who do their good works to bring attention to themselves show they lack proper knowledge. Those who continue to belittle those who don't minister the way they do most likely are battling pride.

My prayer for us today is: "If any of you lacks wisdom, let him ask of God, who gives to all liberally and without reproach, and it will be given to him." James 1:5

DAY 109

Fervent & Earnest Prayer

"Confess your trespasses to one another, and pray for one another, that you may be healed. The effective, fervent prayer of a righteous man avails much. Elijah was a man with a nature like ours, and he prayed earnestly that it would not rain; and it did not rain on the land for three years and six months. And he prayed again, and the heaven gave rain, and the earth produced its fruit." James 5:16-18

The only thing unchangeable in this world is God Almighty Himself, who said, "For I am the LORD; I do not change" (Malachi 3:6). Everything else is subject to change, especially when God's people fervently pray in faith and the LORD responds.

The idea of fervent in this context is strong. It is rendered: Very strong in the supplication of a righteous man, energizing. In other words, effective prayer must be fervent, not because we must emotionally persuade a reluctant God, but because we must gain God's heart by being fervent for the things He is.

Elijah was a man who faced temptations and human frailties just like you and me, but he walked in the supernatural. Elijah found such favor with God that God carried him supernaturally to Heaven in a chariot of fire when he finished his time in this world. How did Elijah become such a history-maker and world changer? The scriptures give us the answer, "He prayed earnestly" (v. 15).

185

Elijah is a model of earnest prayer that God answered. His effectiveness in prayer extended even to the weather! Yet this shows that Elijah's heart was in tune with God's. He prayed for the rain to stop and start because he sensed it was in the heart of God in His dealings with His people.

My prayer for us today is that we would learn to be fervent and earnest in prayer.

DAY 110

The Way Maker

"No temptation has overtaken you except such as is common to man; but God is faithful, who will not allow you to be tempted beyond what you are able, but with the temptation will also make the way of escape, that you may be able to bear it." 1 Corinthians 10:13

Notice how the "way of escape" does not lead us to a place where we escape all temptation (that is heaven alone). The way of escape leads us to the place where we may be able to bear it. Also, in Matthew 4, we read how the devil temps Jesus: "Now when the tempter came to Him, he said, "If You are the Son of God, command that these stones become bread." Matthew 4:3

"And said to Him, 'If You are the Son of God, throw Yourself down. For it is written: He shall give His angels charge over you,' and, 'in their hands, they shall bear you up, Lest you dash your foot against a stone.'" Matthew 4:6

"Again, the devil took Him up on an exceedingly high mountain and showed Him all the kingdoms of the world and their glory. And he said to Him, "All these things I will give You if You will fall down and worship me." Matthew 4:8-9

What I notice in temptation is the devil's desire to cause you to doubt "who" and "whose" you are—in other words, questioning your sense of belonging and God's ability to provide for you.

187

My prayer for us today is that we recognize our Faithful Father as the Way Maker. Believing that we are His children and that all we need is found in HIM. "But as many as received Him, to them He gave the right to become children of God, to those who believe in His name: who were born, not of blood, nor of the will of the flesh, nor of the will of man, but of God." John 1:12-13

DAY 111

The Free Gift

"And the gift is not like that which came through the one who sinned. For the judgment which came from one offense resulted in condemnation, but the free gift which came from many offenses resulted in justification." Romans 5:16

From this passage, Adam and Jesus are sometimes known as the two men. Between them, they represent all humanity, and everyone is identified in either Adam or Jesus. We are born identified with Adam; we may be born again into identification with Jesus (see John 3:3). If we choose Adam, we receive judgment and condemnation. If we choose Jesus, we receive a free gift of God's grace that leads to justification. Justification is an image from the court of law. Justification solves the problem of man's guilt before a righteous Judge.

We need to take a close look into what this "free gift" accomplished. Adam gave an offense that had consequences for the entire human race – as a result of Adam's transgression, many died. Jesus gives a free gift that has implications for the whole human race but in a different way. Through the free gift of Jesus, the grace of God abounded to many. Adam's work brought death, but Jesus' work brings grace that leads to justification.

My prayer for us today is that we rejoice in this free gift: "For by grace you have been saved through faith, and that not of yourselves; it is the gift of God," Ephesians 2:8

DAY 112

Do Not Worry

"But seek first the kingdom of God and His righteousness, and all these things shall be added to you. Therefore do not worry about tomorrow, for tomorrow will worry about its own things. Sufficient for the day is its own trouble."
Matthew 6:33-34

Did you know that the word "worry" comes from the Old English root word, "wyrgan," which meant "to strangle" or "to choke"? Worry squeezes the life out of us. Jesus said, "And which of you by being anxious can add a single hour to his span of life?…Therefore, do not be anxious about tomorrow, for tomorrow will be anxious for itself. Sufficient for the day is its own trouble" (Matthew 6:27, 34 ESV).

One of my heroes, Corrie ten Boom, put it this way, "Worrying doesn't empty tomorrow of its sorrow; it empties today of its strength." So, how should we respond to our present struggles? Replace worry with faith. We must "…fix [our] thoughts on what is true, and honorable, and right, and pure, and lovely, and admirable. Think about things that are excellent and worthy of praise" as the apostle Paul tells us in Philippians 4:8 (NLT). These are eight different kinds of things we can fill our minds with that will transform our thinking!

We can also pray for others. Pray for those who are sick, pray for those at risk, pray for the doctors, nurses, and researchers treating patients. Pray for church leaders and government officials who have to make difficult decisions, and pray for your friends, family members, and neighbors. Thinking about others takes the focus off of ourselves and helps to reduce our worry and anxiety!

My prayer for us today is: "Cast your burden on the LORD, And He shall sustain you; He shall never permit the righteous to be moved." Psalm 55:2

DAY 113

The LORD Is My Shepherd

"The LORD is my shepherd; I shall not want." Psalms 23:1

In the New Testament, Jesus announced Himself as the "good Shepherd." He said it so plainly there could be no mistake what He meant. He fulfills the ideal of shepherd-like care for the people of God, as illustrated in the Old Testament.

"I am the good shepherd; and I know My sheep, and am known by My own. As the Father knows Me, even so I know the Father; and I lay down My life for the sheep." John 10:14-15

The good shepherd lives and dies for the good of the sheep. In other words, the Good Shepherd sacrifices for the sheep. The Good Shepherd knows his sheep ("I know My sheep"). We may think of people as the same, but the Good Shepherd knows they are individuals with their personalities and characteristics. As followers of Christ, we believe in the promise and fulfillment of Scripture: "He will feed His flock like a shepherd; He will gather the lambs with His arm, And carry them in His bosom, And gently lead those who are with young." Isaiah 40:11

Today, I pray that we find Jesus to be the Shepherd that He is so that we do not want (or lack for what is needed).

DAY 114

He Himself Will Rule

"He was clothed with a robe dipped in blood, and His name is called The Word of God. And the armies in heaven, clothed in fine linen, white and clean, followed Him on white horses. Now out of His mouth goes a sharp sword, that with it He should strike the nations. And He Himself will rule them with a rod of iron. He Himself treads the winepress of the fierceness and wrath of Almighty God. And He has on His robe and on His thigh a name written: KING OF KINGS AND LORD OF LORDS." Revelation 19:13-16

When Jesus Christ returns, every earthly (former and present) king, president, prime minister, ambassador, members of Congress, senator, judge, priest, and a minister will give account to the KING OF KINGS AND LORD OF LORDS. But, unfortunately, the earthly rulers who are motivated by envy, hatred, and deceit don't understand or even comprehend the responsibility they have in giving an account to the One who rules with a rod of iron.

Jesus comes to rule, reign in triumph, and rule the nations with a rod of iron as predicted in Psalm 2. He comes as King of Kings to displace every king reigning on this earth. Until the return of Christ, we will have to endure temporary (not eternal) acts of injustice, manipulation, and divisiveness. However, remember, these plans will not last forever. "While we do not look at the things which are seen, but at the things which are not seen. For the things which are seen are temporary, but the things which are not seen are eternal." 2 Corinthians 4:18

It's good for us to remember that this dramatic display of judgment comes only at the end of a long time of grace, patience, and mercy. This promise is no "rush to judgment." Jesus has amply displayed His nature of long-suffering (see 2 Peter 3:8-9) to this fallen world. He comes now to judge a world hardened to their rebellion against Him.

My prayer for us today is that we would have a greater understanding of the power and authority of Jesus Christ and look forward to HIS return.

DAY 115

Your Advantage

"Nevertheless I tell you the truth. It is to your advantage that I go away; for if I do not go away, the Helper will not come to you; but if I depart, I will send Him to you." John 16:7

For the disciples, at this time, it was difficult for them to see any advantages: For example, all they could see was:
  · How is it an advantage that Jesus is arrested?
  · How is it an advantage that Jesus' ministry of teaching and miracles is stopped?
  · How is it an advantage that Jesus is beaten?
  · How is it an advantage that Jesus is mocked?
  · How is it an advantage that Jesus is sentenced for execution?
  · How is it an advantage that Jesus is nailed to a cross?
  · How is it an advantage that Jesus dies in the company of notorious criminals?

But, despite all of that, He wanted them to know that it was to their advantage. What are the benefits of the coming of the Holy Spirit?:

1.   He Helps - Romans 8:26
2.   He guides - John 16:13
3.   He teaches - John 14:26
4.   He speaks - Revelation 2:7
5.   He reveals - 1 Corinthians 2:10
6.   He instructs - Acts 8:26
7.   He testifies of Jesus Christ - John 15:26

8. He comforts - Acts 9:11
9. He calls - Acts 13:2
10. He fills - Acts 4:31
11. He strengthens - Ephesians 3:16
12. He prays - Romans 8:26
13. He prophecies through us - 2 Peter 1:21
14. He bears witness of the truth - Romans 9:1
15. He brings joy - 1 Thessalonians 1:6
16. He brings freedom - 2 Corinthians 3:17
17. He helps us obey - 1 Peter 1:22
18. He calls for Jesus' return - Revelation 22:17
19. He lives in us - 1 Corinthians 3:16
20. He frees us - Romans 8:2

My prayer for us today is that we recognize the advantage: "And the disciples were filled with joy and with the Holy Spirit." Acts 13:52

DAY 116

Caring For One Another

"And in these days prophets came from Jerusalem to Antioch. Then one of them, named Agabus, stood up and showed by the Spirit that there was going to be a great famine throughout all the world, which also happened in the days of Claudius Caesar. Then the disciples, each according to his ability, determined to send relief to the brethren dwelling in Judea. This they also did, and sent it to the elders by the hands of Barnabas and Saul." Acts 11:27-30

We don't know exactly how the Prophet Agabus "showed by the Spirit" there was going to be a great famine throughout the world, but we know the Christians took the word seriously and generously prepared to meet the coming need.

Difficult times are among us today. However, Christians are CALLED to Shine in the Darkness. Christians are CALLED to Shine in Famine. Christians are CALLED to Shine in Persecution. Christians are called to share and care for one another.

How?
1. Positioned to hear God's Word through the various channels He uses (Acts 11:27-28).
2. Willing to respond to the needs of God's people (Acts 11:29).
3. Ready to fulfill your ministry (Acts 11:30; 12:25).
4. Be sent out by the Holy Spirit (Acts 13:2, 4).

My prayer for us today is that we have God's heart to care for one another: "You did not choose Me, but I chose you and appointed you that you should go and bear fruit, and that your fruit should remain, that whatever you ask the Father in My name He may give you. These things I command you, that you love one another." John 15:16-17

DAY 117

Savior of the World

"And we have seen and testify that the Father has sent the Son as Savior of the world. Whoever confesses that Jesus is the Son of God, God abides in him, and he in God." 1 John 4:14-15

Jesus wasn't just the Jewish Messiah. He was the Savior of the world! And for those who sincerely confess Jesus as the Son of God, the reward is glorious, God abides in him, and he in God.

The Apostle John clarifies that it isn't enough to have knowledge and facts about who Jesus is; we must confess the truth. The idea behind the word "confess" is to be in agreement with. We must agree with God about who Jesus is. We are called to confess that Jesus is the Son of God, from our hearts: "that if you confess with your mouth the Lord Jesus and believe in your heart that God has raised Him from the dead, you will be saved. For with the heart, one believes unto righteousness, and with the mouth, confession is made unto salvation. For the Scripture says, "Whoever believes on Him will not be put to shame....For 'whoever calls on the name of the LORD shall be saved.'" Romans 10:9-11, 13

When we confess... the Lord Jesus, we agree with what God said about Jesus and with what Jesus said about Himself. It means we recognize that Jesus is God, that He is the Messiah and Savior of the world, and that His work on the cross is the only way of salvation for humanity.

Today, my prayer is that our mouth continues to confess Jesus Christ as LORD because our hearts are bursting with gratitude for HIS salvation.

DAY 118

Make Disciples

"And Jesus came and spoke to them, saying, "All authority has been given to Me in heaven and on earth. Go therefore and make disciples of all the nations, baptizing them in the name of the Father and of the Son and of the Holy Spirit, teaching them to observe all things that I have commanded you; and lo, I am with you always, even to the end of the age." Amen." Matthew 28:18-20

Because Jesus has this authority, we are therefore commanded to go. His authority sends us, His power guides us, and His reign empowers us. His work and message would continue to the world through His disciples. The command is to make disciples, and it is not merely to convert or support a cause. The idea behind the word disciples is of scholars, learners, or students. Making disciples reminds us that disciples are made. Disciples are not spontaneously created at conversion; they are the product of a process involving other Believers.

Here are some practical first steps in the discipleship process:
1) Give someone you've witnessed to a Bible, and suggest a reading plan (I usually start with the book of Mark or John);
2) Schedule regular times to meet, individually or with a small group;
3) Feed your disciples regularly with simple Bible truths (through meetings, calls, or texts);
4) Talk to them about water baptism and schedule this;

201

5) Get your disciple connected to a church so they can have regular fellowship.

Paul viewed new believers as infants, and he nurtured them "as a nursing mother tenderly cares for her own children" (1 Thessalonians 2:7). Be attentive, caring, and focused on a disciple's growth.

My prayer for us today is that we continue to walk in the authority that has been given, to make disciples who eventually make disciples too.

DAY 119

Take My Yoke

"Come to Me, all you who labor and are heavy laden, and I will give you rest. Take My yoke upon you and learn from Me, for I am gentle and lowly in heart, and you will find rest for your souls. For My yoke is easy and My burden is light."
Matthew 11:28-30

According to Theologians, the ancient Jews commonly used the idea of the yoke to express someone's obligation to God. Thus, there was the yoke of the law, the yoke of the commands, the yoke of repentance, the yoke of faith, and the general yoke of God. In this context, it is easy to see Jesus simplifying and saying, "Forget about all those other yokes. Instead, take My yoke upon you and learn from Me."

· The yoke of Jesus is easy and light as compared with the yoke   of others.
· The yoke of Jesus is easy and light as long as we do not rebel   against it.
· The yoke of Jesus has nothing to do with worries and anxieties that lead us to fear.
· The yoke of Jesus does not include the burdens we choose to add to it.

Jesus described His gift to His followers as rest for your soul. Similar words can be found in the Hebrew text of Jeremiah 6:16, where it is the offer of God to those who follow His way; Jesus now issues the invitation in His name!" Jesus summarized this wonderful call with this assurance. The yoke is easy, and the burden is light because He bears it with us. Held alone leads to weariness and discouragement, but with Jesus, it can be easy and light.

My prayer for us today is that we see Jesus in His rightful place. "And Jesus came and spoke to them, saying, "All authority has been given to Me in heaven and on earth." Matthew 28:18

DAY 120

Humility and The Fear of the LORD

"By humility and the fear of the LORD Are riches and honor and life." Proverbs 22:4

The two major themes which are interwoven and overlapping throughout Proverbs are wisdom and folly. Wisdom, which includes knowledge, understanding, instruction, discretion, and obedience, is built on the fear of the Lord and the Word of God. Folly is everything opposite to wisdom. Folly will keep us from experiencing riches, honor, and life.

Most of us would like to enjoy the fruit and blessings of riches, honor, and life. However, the combinations of these blessings are the buy products of humility and fear of the Lord. These two qualities are connected. Humility is a good view of self; fear of the Lord is an appropriate view of God. When we have these two principles working in us, we are well on our way to the path of wisdom that leads to riches, honor, and life.

My prayer for us today is that we walk in humility and the fear of the Lord. May we recognize that without HIM we can do nothing. "I am the vine, you are the branches. He who abides in Me, and I in him, bears much fruit; for without Me you can do nothing." John 15:5

DAY 121

What The LORD Hates

"These six things the LORD hates, Yes, seven are an abomination to Him: A proud look, A lying tongue, Hands that shed innocent blood, A heart that devises wicked plans, Feet that are swift in running to evil, A false witness who speaks lies, And one who sows discord among brethren."
Proverbs 6:16-19

These are strong words that we read in the book of proverbs. Since the "LORD" reveals His heart towards "these things," we should take them very seriously. But, to say the least, we do not want them to be a part of our life in any way. Avoiding what God hates and considers an abomination requires the following:

1. Walking humbly before God.
2. Speaking truth to others.
3. Loving our neighbor.
4. Finding ways to bless one another.
5. Being a peacemaker.
6. Having grace in our speech.
7. Praying for unity as Jesus did in John 17

My prayer for us today is that we ask God to lead us in the way of everlasting. "Search me, O God, and know my heart; Try me, and know my anxieties; And see if there is any wicked way in me, And lead me in the way everlasting."
Psalm 139:23-24

DAY 122

Love Suffers Long

"Love suffers long and is kind; love does not envy; love does not parade itself, is not puffed up; does not behave rudely, does not seek its own, is not provoked, thinks no evil;" 1 Corinthians 13:4-5

These verses remind us that Love is longsuffering and powerful. It is the heart demonstrated in God when He says, "The Lord is not slack concerning His promise, as some count slackness, but is longsuffering toward us, not willing that any should perish but that all should come to repentance" (2 Peter 3:9). The truth is, if God's Love is in us, we will show longsuffering to those who annoy us and even those who hurt us.

Two of my favorite quotes: Martin Luther King, Jr. said,

"I refuse to accept the view that mankind is so tragically bound to the starless midnight of racism and war that the bright daybreak of peace and brotherhood can never become a reality… I believe that unarmed truth and unconditional Love will have the final word. We must develop and maintain the capacity to forgive. He who is devoid of the power to forgive is devoid of the power to love. There is some good in the worst of us and some evil in the best of us. When we discover this, we are less prone to hate our enemies."

"Darkness cannot drive out darkness; only light can do that. Hate cannot drive out hate; only Love can do that."

207

Lastly, Love... does not rejoice in iniquity: It desires the best for others and refuses to color things against others. Instead, Love rejoices in the truth. Therefore, Love can always stand with and on truth because Love is pure and good.

My prayer for us today is that we experience the power of Love even when darkness is all around us.

DAY 123

The CARE of the Shepherd

*"I am the good shepherd. The good shepherd gives His life for the sheep. But a hireling, he who is not the shepherd, one who does not own the sheep, sees the wolf coming and leaves the sheep and flees; and the wolf catches the sheep and scatters them. The hireling flees because he is a hireling and does not **care** about the sheep. I am the good shepherd; and I know My sheep, and am known by My own. As the Father knows Me, even so I know the Father; and I lay down My life for the sheep. And other sheep I have which are not of this fold; them also I must bring, and they will hear My voice; and there will be one flock and one shepherd." John 10:11-16*

We see in these verses that the "hireling," who does not care, will not defend the sheep. However, the Good Shepherd lives and dies for the good of the sheep. The Good Shepherd sacrifices for the sheep (gives His life). The Good Shepherd knows his sheep (I know My sheep). We think sheep are all the same; however, the Shepherd knows they are individuals with personalities and characteristics. The sheep know the Good Shepherd.

I've come up with an acronym about our Great Shepherd who CARES:

C - Comfort (comes along side) 2 Corinthians 1:3
A - Abundant (abundant life) John 10:10
R - Resurrection (living hope) 1 Peter 1:3
E - Eternity (eternal life) Ephesians 3:10-11

S - Success (blessings, favor) Joshua 1:8

The life of Christ Jesus demonstrates He cares. It is for us He lives, and because He lives, we live also. Jesus lives to represent us to the Father. He CARES!

My prayer for us today is that we know that God cares: "Casting all your care upon Him, for He cares for you." 1 Peter 5:7

DAY 124

Knowledge of the Truth

"Who desires all men to be saved and to come to the knowledge of the truth." 1 Timothy 2:4

It is clear from this verse that God desires all men to be saved. However, God's desire for all to be saved is conditioned by His desire to have a genuine response from human beings. In other words, He won't fulfill His desire to save all men at the expense of making men robots that worship Him from being programmed to do so. This acknowledgment of Him is why faith pleases God. When we receive God's gift and act upon it, we are fulfilling God's desire (Hebrews 11:6). Salvation, God's free gift, is associated with coming to the knowledge of the truth. One cannot be saved apart from excepting who Jesus (Yeshua) is and what He has done to save us. The Apostle Paul is simply echoing what Jesus said in John 14:6: Jesus said to him, "I am the way, the truth, and the life. No one comes to the Father except through Me."

Remember, Jesus didn't say that He would show us a way; He said He is the way. He didn't promise to teach us the truth; He said that He is the truth. Jesus didn't offer us the secrets to life; He said that He is the life.

My prayer for us today is that we come to the knowledge of the truth by receiving Jesus (Yeshua) as our LORD and SAVIOR.

DAY 125

Answers from the Book of Genesis

"So God created man in His own image; in the image of God He created him; male and female He created them." Genesis *1:27*

In this book, we find the answer to how our world came to be. First, God created the earth and everything in it and made man in His image. Second, we also learn that when God created Adam and Eve, they were without sin. But they became sinful when they disobeyed God and ate some fruit from the tree: "but of the tree of the knowledge of good and evil you shall not eat, for in the day that you eat of it you shall surely die (Genesis 2:17).

Through Adam and Eve, we learn about the destructive power of sin and its bitter consequences. When we disobey our Creator, we ruin our lives with sin. But, the opposite is true; when we live as God intended, life becomes fruitful and fulfilling.

God makes a promise to help and protect humanity. This kind of promise is called a "covenant." The only way to enjoy the benefits of God's promises is to, by faith, believe in Him: "just as Abraham "believed God, and it was accounted to him for righteousness." Therefore know that only those who are of faith are sons of Abraham. And the Scripture, foreseeing that God would justify the Gentiles by faith, preached the gospel to Abraham beforehand, saying, "In you all the nations shall be blessed." So then those who are of faith are blessed with believing Abraham." Galatians 3:6-9

When people, by faith, believe in God, they find peace with their Creator, love for others, and joy within themselves. Simply put, the purpose of this book is to record God's creation of the world and to reveal His desire to have a people set apart to worship (obey) Him. God would have us be blessed so that we would become a blessing: "I will make you a great nation; I will bless you And make your name great; And you shall be a blessing. I will bless those who bless you, And I will curse him who curses you; And in you all the families of the earth shall be blessed."" Genesis 12:2-3

My prayer for us today is that we would be blessed with answers as we read and study the book of Genesis.

DAY 126

He Appointed

"Then He appointed twelve, that they might be with Him and that He might send them out to preach, and to have power to heal sicknesses and to cast out demons:" Mark 3:14-15

He called the twelve from among His larger circle of followers, and He appointed them that they might be with Him. The first job of the disciples was to be with Jesus, to learn from being around Him, in what they heard and witnessed through Him. Then, in a secondary sense, He chose them that He might send them out to preach. This calling needs to remind us that we will only be as fruitful or valuable to the degree we have "been with" Jesus. The truth be known, little is done for the glory of God by those who preach without having a personal relationship with Jesus Christ. In other words, you have nothing to give apart from what you have received by spending time with Jesus.

When someone has been with Jesus and is commissioned, they can expect that Jesus will give them the power to serve, including seeing miraculous works (heal sicknesses and cast our demons) done in their commissioning. The very heart of Jesus is to see people saved, healed, and delivered from the enemy's plot. "Heal the sick, cleanse the lepers, raise the dead, cast out demons. Freely you have received, freely give." Matthew 10:8

Our prayer for you today is that you would embrace all that is part of your appointment. "And they went out and preached

214

everywhere, the Lord working with them and confirming the word through the accompanying signs. Amen." Mark 16:20

DAY 127

He Who Is Of God Hears God's Words

"Why do you not understand My speech? Because you are not able to listen to My word. You are of your father the devil, and the desires of your father you want to do. He was a murderer from the beginning, and does not stand in the truth, because there is no truth in him. When he speaks a lie, he speaks from his own resources, for he is a liar and the father of it. But because I tell the truth, you do not believe Me. Which of you convicts Me of sin? And if I tell the truth, why do you not believe Me? He who is of God hears God's words; therefore you do not hear, because you are not of God." John 8:43-47

Notice how Jesus asked a question (Why do you not understand My speech?), and then answered (Because you cannot listen to My word.) The religious leaders brought up the issue of bloodline by insulting Jesus in John 8:41. Jesus replied by explaining their spiritual ancestry. He was very blunt, and they were the spiritual children of the devil. This statement was evident in that their desires matched the devil's desire to kill and deceive.

Jesus gives us some insights into the character of Satan. First, the lie is core to the devil's character, and he is the deceiver who has deceived himself and others.

But because I tell you the truth, you do not believe Me: They rejected Jesus because He told them the truth they did not want to hear. It was not because He spoke lies. Again, Jesus allowed His enemies – who hated Him so badly they wanted to kill Him – to declare some sin in Him – and they could not. This fact was another remarkable testimony to the sinlessness of Jesus Christ.

My prayer for us today is that we would hear, accept, and obey God's Word. "Then the righteous will shine forth as the sun in the kingdom of their Father. He who has ears to hear, let him hear!" Matthew 13:43

DAY 128

He Will Not Leave You

"Be strong and of good courage, do not fear nor be afraid of them; for the LORD your God, He is the One who goes with you. He will not leave you nor forsake you."
Deuteronomy 31:6

I don't claim to know all that is ahead of us in the days to come. But this one thing I believe we can be assured of, that God Himself has gone before us and will also walk with us. We need not fear because we are not alone. As a small child, I remember singing an old hymn of the church. The chorus reads like this:

No Never alone, No Never alone,
He promised Never to leave us, Never to leave me alone;
No, never alone, No, never alone,
He promised never to leave me, Never to leave me alone.

Holding onto the promises of God is very important. For example: "Fear not, for I am with you; Be not dismayed, for I am your God. I will strengthen you, Yes, I will help you, I will uphold you with My righteous right hand." Isaiah 41:10

My prayer for us today is that we would have the assurance of HIS presence in our lives. "May the LORD our God be with us, as He was with our fathers. May He not leave us nor forsake us," 1 Kings 8:57

DAY 129

Come & Eat

"Jesus said to them, 'Come and eat breakfast.' Yet none of the disciples dared ask Him, 'Who are You?'—knowing that it was the Lord. Jesus then came and took the bread and gave it to them, and likewise the fish." John 21:12-13

I recently read a survey on what Americans longed to hear above anything else. The three top answers were the following: "I love you," I forgive you," and "Suppers ready." The first two longings do not surprise me because we desperately need love and forgiveness. However, the third longing is the most interesting to me today as I read the scriptures.

I continue to be amazed at these words: Jesus said to them, "Come and eat breakfast": What stands out to me is the servant nature of Jesus, even in His resurrection. He prepared breakfast for His disciples, and no doubt a delicious one. The desire of Jesus to make breakfast for the disciples speaks of fellowship and depth of relationship. He knows the longings of our hearts.

My prayer for us today is that we hear and embrace the words of Jesus when He says, "Behold, I stand at the door and knock. If anyone hears My voice and opens the door, I will come in to him and dine with him, and he with Me." Revelation 3:20

DAY 130

Such A High Priest

"For such a High Priest was fitting for us, who is holy, harmless, undefiled, separate from sinners, and has become higher than the heavens; who does not need daily, as those high priests, to offer up sacrifices, first for His own sins and then for the people's, for this He did once for all when He offered up Himself. For the law appoints as high priests men who have weakness, but the word of the oath, which came after the law, appoints the Son who has been perfected forever." Hebrews 7:26-28

I love this statement, "For such a High Priest was fitting for us." In other words, the priests under the Law of Moses did not have the personal character of the Son of God. Jesus is holy, harmless (without guile or deception), undefiled, separate from sinners (in the sense of not sharing in their sin). Jesus is far superior in His character to any earthly priest.

The truth is, God didn't have confidence in man to obey the Law and find righteousness through keeping the Law. This fact is the reason He provided for the sacrifice - the punishment of a perfect, innocent victim in the place of the sinner. God did not expect an Israelite to trust in his obedience to the Law to save Him (though God wanted Israel to love His Law). Instead, God expected an Israelite to trust in the atonement made by sacrifice to make him righteous and understand that this sacrifice pointed towards a perfect gift God would one day make through the Son of Man, the Messiah.

220

My prayer for us today is that we rejoice in God's provision: "Therefore, brethren, having boldness to enter the Holiest by the blood of Jesus, by a new and living way which He consecrated for us, through the veil, that is, His flesh, and having a High Priest over the house of God, let us draw near with a true heart in full assurance of faith, having our hearts sprinkled from an evil conscience and our bodies washed with pure water." Hebrews 10:19-22

DAY 131

Not Seeking My Own

*"Therefore, whether you eat or drink, or whatever you do, do all to the glory of God. Give no offense, either to the Jews or to the Greeks or to the church of God, just as I also please all men in all things, **not seeking my own** profit, but the profit of many, that they may be saved." 1 Corinthians 10:31-33*

This passage can be a fresh reminder that the purpose of our lives isn't to see how self-centered or self-absorbed we can become. Nor is it to see how much we can get away with and still be Christians; instead, it is to develop the very heart of God for others so that we might serve the LORD by serving others.

For example, Jesus teaches how He will judge the nations: "for I was hungry and you gave Me food; I was thirsty and you gave Me drink; I was a stranger and you took Me in; I was naked and you clothed Me; I was sick and you visited Me; I was in prison and you came to Me. Then the righteous will answer Him, saying, 'Lord, when did we see You hungry and feed You, or thirsty and give You drink? When did we see You a stranger and take You in, or naked and clothe You? Or when did we see You sick, or in prison, and come to You?' And the King will answer and say to them, 'Assuredly, I say to you, inasmuch as you did it to one of the least of these My brethren, you did it to Me.'" Matthew 25:35-40

Notice how giving to others keeps you from being self-centered, and more importantly, keeps you in the heart of God.

My prayer for us today is: "Let each of you look out not only for his own interests, but also for the interests of others." Philippians 2:4

DAY 132

By the Grace of God I am what I am

"But by the grace of God I am what I am, and His grace toward me was not in vain; but I labored more abundantly than they all, yet not I, but the grace of God which was with me." 1 Corinthians 15:10

Do you need a change in your life? Do you want to see a difference in your family? Well, it can happen when you look to the grace of God. The Apostle Paul gave the grace of God all the credit for the change in His life. He was a changed man, forgiven, cleansed, and full of love when he used to be full of hate. He knew this was not his accomplishment, but it was the work of the grace of God in him. The grace that saves us also changes us. Grace changed Paul. The truth is, you can't receive the grace of God without being changed by it. However, some changes don't always come all at once. And some changes won't be complete until we pass to the next life. However, the truth be known, we are being changed: "But whenever someone turns to the Lord, the veil is taken away...So all of us who have had that veil removed can see and reflect the glory of the Lord. And the Lord—who is the Spirit—makes us more and more like Him as we are changed into His glorious image." 2 Corinthians 3:16, 18 NLT

My prayer for us today is that we can also say, "by the grace of God I am what I am."

DAY 133

The God Of Relationship

"Moreover God said to Moses, 'Thus you shall say to the children of Israel: 'The LORD God of your fathers, the God of Abraham, the God of Isaac, and the God of Jacob, has sent me to you. This is My name forever, and this is My memorial to all generations.'" Exodus 3:15

At the burning bush, God revealed Himself to Moses as "the God of Abraham, the God of Isaac, and Jacob." This declaration should amaze us all. Why would the perfect and flawless Creator of Heaven name Himself with the names of imperfect and flawed men? Could it be by doing so, God is showing that He is not a distant God who is relationally uninvolved in the lives of His people. Instead, the Creator of the heavens and earth holds a very personal love toward any individual with whom He has a genuine relationship.

May you be encouraged knowing that He is not just the God of the universe; He is the God who embraces people. He is not just the God of a nation of nameless faces; He is the Creator of every person.

My prayer for us today is that we would know His desire for relationship: "He who believes in the Son of God has the witness in himself; he who does not believe God has made Him a liar, because he has not believed the testimony that God has given of His Son. And this is the testimony: that God has given us eternal life, and this life is in His Son. He who has the Son has life; he who does not have the Son of God does not have life. These things I have written to you who believe in the name of the Son of God, that you may know that you have eternal life, and that you may continue to believe in the name of the Son of God." 1 John 5:10-13

DAY 134

Holiness

"Be Holy because I, the LORD your God, am holy." Leviticus 19:2

The Book of Leviticus begins where the Book of Exodus ends, at the foot of Mount Sinai. The tabernacle was just completed (Exodus 35-40), and God was now positioning the people to learn how to worship there. This instruction was a handbook for the priest and Levites outlining their duties in worship and a guidebook for holy living for the Hebrews.

The overall theme or message of Leviticus is the holiness of God. However, there is a question, "How can an unholy people approach a Holy God?" The answer - the first sin must be dealt with in man. This theme becomes the opening chapter of the book of Leviticus as it gives detailed instructions for offering sacrifices, which were the active symbols of repentance and obedience. Offerings of bulls, grain, goats, or sheep had to be perfect, with no defects or bruises. This instruction became the picture of the ultimate sacrifice to come, Jesus the Lamb of God.

Jesus has come and opened the way to God by giving up His life as the final sacrifice in our place. True worship and oneness (relationship) with God begins as we confess our sin and accept Christ as the only one who can redeem us from sin and help us approach a Holy God.

The Holiness of Christ redeems us and positions us so we can glorify the LORD. Paul developed this same line of thought in 1 Corinthians 6:9-11 and 6:15-20, concluding with the idea that we should glorify God in our body and in our spirit, which is God's.

My prayer for us today is that our relationship with Jesus would cause us to say: "For God did not call us to uncleanness, but in holiness. 1 Thessalonians 4:7

DAY 135

Wisdom Warning

*"Who is wise and understanding among you? Let him show by good conduct that his works are done in the meekness of wisdom. But if you have bitter envy and self-seeking in your hearts, do not boast and lie against the truth. This **wisdom** does not descend from above, but is earthly, sensual, demonic. For where envy and self-seeking exist, confusion and every evil thing are there." James 3:13-16*

"**This wisdom**" that James referred to was not really wisdom at all. It is the wisdom claimed by the would-be teachers of James 3:14 whose lives contradict their claims. Such 'wisdom' evaluates everything by worldly standards and makes personal gain life's highest goal. They show a **wisdom** that is **earthly, sensual**, and **demonic**. Their wisdom is more characteristic of the world, the flesh, and the devil than of God. This is the fruit of human effort, it may be able to accomplish things, but with the ultimate fruit of **confusion and every evil thing**. It is clear from the Book of James that wisdom is not mere head knowledge. Real wisdom and **understanding** will show in our lives, by our **good conduct** that accomplishes the will of God.

My prayer for us today is: "See then that you walk circumspectly, not as fools but as wise, redeeming the time, because the days are evil. Therefore do not be unwise, but understand what the will of the Lord is." Ephesians 5:15-17

DAY 136

Praise Is Pleasant & Beautiful

"Praise the LORD! For it is good to sing praises to our God; For it is pleasant, and praise is beautiful." Psalm 147:1

The Psalmist is not suggesting praise in this verse, he is rather declaring its significance. Praising the LORD is pleasant and beautiful because it is proclaiming truth. Let's face it, the more you watch the news, the media coverage of politics, the more you witness that which is not so pleasant or beautiful. It's no wonder that God commanded "praise." HE knows that we need it. We need to experience what is pleasant and beautiful. When we follow this instruction we won't remain weary and discouraged in the journey of life. When we follow this commend we defeat the temptation to waste our life in temporary circumstances.

It is good to praise the LORD because it is right; good because it is acceptable with God, beneficial to ourselves, and edifying in our fellowship with others. Singing HIS praises is the best possible use of speech: it speaks of God, for God, and to God, and it does this in a joyful and reverent manner. Simply put, It is pleasant and proper, sweet and suitable to sing Hallelujah to the Lord Most High. Praise is something we engage in that has eternal meaning.

My prayer for us today is that we: "Praise the LORD, for the LORD is good; Sing praises to His name, for it is pleasant." Psalm 135:3

DAY 137

The Kingdom of God

"And Jesus went about all Galilee, teaching in their synagogues, preaching the gospel of the kingdom, and healing all kinds of sickness and all kinds of disease among the people." Matthew 4:23

Jesus came into the world and preached the Kingdom of God. This proclamation gives the message of the "Kingdom" its significance. Here are some other examples:

1. Provision is found in the Kingdom: "But seek the kingdom of God, and all these things shall be added to you." Luke 12:31
2. Righteousness, peace, and joy are found in the Kingdom:" for the Kingdom of God is not eating and drinking, but righteousness and peace and joy in the Holy Spirit." Romans 14:17
3. Power is found in the Kingdom: "For the kingdom of God is not in word but in power." 1 Corinthians 4:20
4. Deliverance is found in the Kingdom: " But if I cast out demons by the Spirit of God, surely the kingdom of God has come upon you." Matt. 12:28
5. New Birth is found in the Kingdom: "Jesus answered and said to him, "Most assuredly, I say to you, unless one is born again, he cannot see the kingdom of God." John 3:3
6. Forever is found in the Kingdom: " And do not lead us into temptation, But deliver us from the evil one.

For Yours is the Kingdom and the power and the glory forever. Amen." Matthew 6:13

7. Prayer is about the Kingdom. That is why we pray: "In this manner, therefore, pray: Our Father in heaven, Hallowed be Your name. Your Kingdom come. Your will be done On earth as it is in heaven." Matthew 6:9-10

My prayer for us today is that the message of the Kingdom will be preached throughout the whole world before the 2nd coming of Christ: "And this gospel of the kingdom will be preached in all the world as a witness to all the nations, and then the end will come." Matthew 24:14

DAY 138

New Creation

"Therefore, if anyone is in Christ, he is a new creation; old things have passed away; behold, all things have become new." 2 Corinthians 5:17

This truth is a promise for anyone. It doesn't matter what class, race, nationality, language, or level of intelligence. Anyone can be a new creation in Jesus Christ. This truth is a promise for anyone who is in Christ. However, this truth is not a promise for those who live for themselves or someone or something else. This truth is for those in Christ. Paul here teaches the great principle of regeneration. Jesus Christ changes those who come to Him by faith and who are in Christ. The saved are not "just forgiven." They are transformed into a new creation. However, being a new creation doesn't mean that we are perfect. It means that we are changed and that we are being changed. Living as a new creation is God's works in us, transforming our mind, will, and emotions. So, we must both receive the gift of being a new creation and be challenged to live the life of a new creation. All this is God's work in us that we submit to in our lives. This truth reminds us that at its root, Christianity is all about what God did for us and our need to walk in it.

Today, I pray that we remember that being a new creation is a gift from God and is received by faith.

DAY 139

His Blessings

"Both riches and honor come from You, And You reign over all. In Your hand is power and might; In Your hand it is to make great And to give strength to all. Now therefore, our God, We thank You And praise Your glorious name."
I Chronicles 29:12-13

King David was able to acknowledge where his blessings came from in his life. We should be thankful for all of our material blessings. Unfortunately, some people are never satisfied with what they have. But what a difference it makes when we realize that everything we have has been given to us by God.

Recently I visited a woman who was wealthy and successful, the envy of friends and business associates. But as we talked, she broke down in tears, confessing that she was miserable inside. Wealth had not been able to fill the empty place in her heart.

Some years ago, I visited a man and woman in Kenya, Africa. Their home was very humble, and they had almost nothing in the way of this world's possessions. Yet their faces were radiant as they told me about the work they were doing for Christ and how Jesus had filled their life with meaning and purpose.

The couple from Africa were the rich people, for they had learned to be thankful for everything God had given them. A spirit of thankfulness makes all the difference.

My prayer for us today is that we can say like Paul, "I have learned the secret of being content in any and every situation, whether well or hungry, whether living in plenty or in want" Philippians 4:12 NIV.

DAY 140

When Kindness Appeared

"But when the kindness and the love of God our Savior toward man appeared, not by works of righteousness which we have done, but according to His mercy He saved us, through the washing of regeneration and renewing of the Holy Spirit, whom He poured out on us abundantly through Jesus Christ our Savior, that having been justified by His grace we should become heirs according to the hope of eternal life." Titus 3:3-7

One thing is for sure. We didn't rescue ourselves. We need to know we were saved by the kindness and the love of God. He reached out to us long before we reached out to Him. Simply put, our lives changed when Jesus Christ made Himself known to us. When we experienced HIS mercy and grace, our thinking and our actions became different. Christ saved us from the inside to the outside.

Remembering this work of God builds four things in us.
　1. Gratitude for how God changed us.
　2. Humility as we see that it was His work that changed us.
　3. Kindness to others in the same place we were.
　4. Faith that God can change those who are still in that place.

Bottom line, when the love of God, our Savior, touches our lives, our dreams change, our motivations change, our attitudes change, our goals change, and our relationships change.

My prayer for us today is that we would know the blessing of being justified by His grace so that we should become heirs according to the hope of eternal life.

DAY 141

Courage

"Have I not commanded you? Be strong and of good courage; do not be afraid, nor be dismayed, for the LORD your God is with you wherever you go." Joshua 1:9

There was a need for such a command because even a great leader like Joshua needed such encouragement.

- Courage is not the absence of fear but the experience of His   strength in the midst of fear.
  -Courage is not self-preservation.
  -Courage is not avoiding conflict or needed conversation.
  -Courage is not lacking a prayer life or study of God's Word.

Rather:
- Courage is giving praise in the midst of the storm.
- Courage is forgiving when you've been wronged.
- Courage is doing the right thing when no one is watching.
- Courage is in everything giving thanks to God, knowing it is   His will to call on Him.
- Courage is finishing the race even if you are in last place.

Lastly:
- It takes brokenness (Repentance) to be saved or converted, but it takes Courage to be a disciple of Christ. - Courage is not just talking about how bad things are in the world but choosing to make a daily difference.

My prayer for you today is that you would: "Be of good courage, And He shall strengthen your heart, All you who hope in the LORD." Psalms 31:24

DAY 142

Don't Let Your Heart Grow Cold

"And because lawlessness will abound, the love of many will grow cold." Matthew 24:12

The devil is the accuser of the brethren, and ultimately he plans to cause the love of many to wax cold. The enemy of our soul would have people alienate themselves and make divisive parties and denominations to keep us suspicious of one another.

How does one's heart grow cold?

1. You think you are wiser than the Word of God so you don't study it (Arrogance).
2. You no longer examine your own heart but rather focus on the faults of others (Self-righteousness).
3. You hold envy and jealousy in your heart (Hatred).
4. You are unwilling to forgive those who hurt you (un-forgiveness).

The answer to lawlessness:

1. **DRAW NEAR TO GOD**
"Let us draw near with a true heart in full assurance of faith, having our hearts sprinkled from an evil conscience and our bodies washed with pure water." Hebrews 10:22

2. **FORGIVE OTHERS**

"For if you forgive men their trespasses, your heavenly Father will also forgive you. But if you do not forgive men their trespasses, neither will your Father forgive your trespasses." Matt. 6:14-15

3. PRAY

"In this manner, therefore, pray: Our Father in heaven, Hallowed be Your name. Your kingdom come. Your will be done On earth as it is in heaven. Give us this day our daily bread. And forgive us our debts, As we forgive our debtors. And do not lead us into temptation, But deliver us from the evil one. For Yours is the kingdom and the power and the glory forever. Amen." Matthew 6:9-13

My prayer for us today is: "For our heart shall rejoice in Him, Because we have trusted in His holy name." Psalm 33:21

DAY 143

A Heart of Thanks

"Therefore be merciful, just as your Father also is merciful."
Luke 6:36
"Blessed are the merciful, For they shall obtain mercy."
Matthew 5:7

I just had the incredible privilege to go around our local hospital and Concord Reserve, A Life Enriching Community, to pray with many nurses. It was National Nurses Week. I am very grateful for the wonderful nurses we have at UH Richmond Heights Medical Center and Concord Reserve in Westlake, OH. Our world is blessed with loving and compassionate people who are making a difference in our communities. May God continue to bless and strengthen the hands of all of our nurses.

A real walk with God shows itself in simple, practical ways. First, it helps the needy and the sick. True religion does not merely give something for the relief of the distressed, but it visits them. It takes them under its care. It goes to their bedside and speaks to their hearts; it relieves their want, sympathizes with them in their distress, instructs them in their care. This care is pure religion found in the love of Christ. This mercy is what I see in the hearts of our nurses.

"Pure and undefiled religion before God and the Father is this: to visit orphans and widows in their trouble...." James 1:27a

To all our nurses out there: A HEART felt THANKS for ALL
that YOU DO!

DAY 144

The Teacher

*"For the Holy Spirit will **teach** you in that very hour what you ought to say.""* Luke 12:12

Whether we realize it or not, we are being taught by someone every day. Education is in the airways, the music, the classroom, the government, the entertainment and sports industry, etc. Teachers are all around us. In some cases, if you don't follow their direction, you are a traitor; you are a socialist; you are a fanatic; you are rightwing; you are leftists; you have a white supremacy problem; you are a hater; you are merciless, and the list goes on and on.

The truth is, where we go for teaching is a matter of spiritual life and death. From the verse above, Luke, the gospel writer, reminds us that in Jesus' departure, He let the disciples know their training was not finished but would continue by the Helper, the Holy Spirit. The Holy Spirit would teach the disciples what more they needed to know and bring to remembrance the words of Jesus. This reminder means that the work of the Spirit would be a work of continuation. His teaching would continue what Jesus already taught.

"But the Helper, the Holy Spirit, whom the Father will send in My name, He will teach you all things, and bring to your remembrance all things that I said to you." John 14:26

The gospel writers remind us that the Holy Spirit would speak to and through us at the crucial moment. The key, however, is

244

that we position ourselves to be a disciple of Christ and receive the Holy Spirit (Acts 8:15).

My prayer for us today is: "But the anointing which you have received from Him abides in you, and you do not need that anyone teach you; but as the same anointing teaches you concerning all things, and is true, and is not a lie, and just as it has taught you, you will abide in Him." 1 John 2:27

DAY 145

Ask, Seek, Knock

"Ask, and it will be given to you; seek, and you will find; knock, and it will be opened to you. For everyone who asks receives, and he who seeks finds, and to him who knocks it will be opened. Or what man is there among you who, if his son asks for bread, will give him a stone? Or if he asks for a fish, will he give him a serpent? If you then, being evil, know how to give good gifts to your children, how much more will your Father who is in heaven give good things to those who ask Him!" Matthew 7:7-11

Ask...seek...knock: We see a progressive fervor, going from asking to seeking to knocking. In other words, Jesus told us to have intensity, passion, and persistence in prayer. The fact that Jesus came back to the subject of prayer after teaching on it already, in some depth in Matthew 6:5-15, shows the importance of prayer. Jesus also made it clear that God doesn't have to be persuaded or appeased in prayer. God promises an answer to the one who diligently asks, seeks, and knocks. He wants to give us not just bread but even more than what we ask for in prayer. However, God values intensity, passion, and persistence in prayer because they show that we share His heart. It shows that we care about the things He cares about in life. It's important to understand that persistent prayer does not overcome God's stubborn reluctance, Rather, it gives glory to Him, expresses dependence upon Him, and aligns our heart more with His.

My prayer for us today is that we:
  1. **Ask** with confidence and humility.
  2. **Seek** wisdom and care.

3. **Knock** with persistence and passion.

DAY 146

Preparation of the Heart

"Then Samuel spoke to all the house of Israel, saying, 'If you return to the LORD with all your hearts, then put away the foreign gods and the Ashtoreths from among you, and prepare your hearts for the LORD, and serve Him only; and He will deliver you from the hand of the Philistines.'"
1 Samuel 7:3

I met someone before the Worldwide Pandemic that made a very impactful statement to me. He said, "If you prepare today, you will not be repairing tomorrow." His point to me was that preparation was vital if you weren't going to repeat past mistakes.

Samuel called the nation to repentance. The repentance had to be inward (with all your hearts) and outward (put away the foreign gods). The inward had to come first. That is why Samuel first called Israel to return with all your hearts, then told them to put away the foreign gods. After the repentance, we read how Israel was called to prepare their hearts. The Israelites preparation of the heart had everything to do with the focus and determination to seek God with all your heart. It was said of King Rehoboam: "And he did evil, because he did not prepare his heart to seek the LORD." 2 Chronicles 12:14

My prayer for us today is that we prepare our hearts to seek the LORD.

DAY 147

Rejoice In The Truth

"Love suffers long and is kind; love does not envy; love does not parade itself, is not puffed up; does not behave rudely, does not seek its own, is not provoked, thinks no evil; ***does not rejoice in iniquity, but rejoices in the truth;"*** *1 Corinthians 13:4-6*

What we find ourselves rejoicing in, or over, tells us a lot about our character. Let's look at another verse that talks about what "not" to rejoice in:

"Do not rejoice when your enemy falls, And do not let your heart be glad when he stumbles; Lest the LORD see it, and it displease Him, And He turn away His wrath from him." Proverbs 24:17-18

It's very clear from these passages of scripture that God wants to teach us what is "not" worth rejoicing in. However, it's not enough to know what we are "not" to rejoice in. We also need to learn what God is rejoicing in and then do the same thing. In other words, what does God want us to rejoice in as we live this life? What moves His heart into rejoicing?

"And when he comes home, he calls together his friends and neighbors, saying to them, 'Rejoice with me, for I have found my sheep which was lost!' I say to you that likewise there will be more joy in heaven over one sinner who repents than over ninety-nine just persons who need no repentance. Luke 15:6-7

"Likewise, I say to you, there is joy in the presence of the angels of God over one sinner who repents." Luke 15:10

"It was right that we should make merry and be glad, for your brother was dead and is alive again, and was lost and is found." Luke 15:32

My prayer for us today is that we learn to rejoice in what God rejoices in - sinners repenting and coming home.

DAY 148

Chosen

"You did not choose Me, but I chose you and appointed you that you should go and bear fruit, and that your fruit should remain, that whatever you ask the Father in My name He may give you. These things I command you, that you love one another." John 15:16-17

Who tells someone they can't be fruitful anymore? One thing for sure, it's not your Heavenly Father! It is apparent in this scripture that HE has chosen you and appointed you to go and bear fruit. Age has no bearing on God's desire to continue to bless you and to bless through you.

Here are some Keys to fruitfulness:
1. Followers of Christ must be rooted in the fact that Jesus chose them, not that they chose Him. In other words, we are in Christ, not because we hold Him, but because He saves us.
2. Jesus chooses disciples not simply so they would have the thrill of knowing they are chosen, but so that they would bear fruit that remains, to the glory of God the Father.
3. Expectation brings about Preparation which causes Equipping for the task of fruitfulness in the Kingdom of God. However, sin and the cares of the world will discourage and destroy our expectations.
4. Fruitfulness is tied to loving one another. In other words, you can't have hate in your heart and remain fruitful.

251

My prayer for us today is that we receive our call to go and bear fruit.

DAY 149

He Is The Strength Of My Heart

"My flesh and my heart fail; But God is the strength of my heart and my portion forever." Psalm 73:26

I find it exciting and encouraging that the Psalmist declares that his flesh and heart fail but emphasizes that God is the "strength of my heart."

The truth is, we all experience at times failings both of flesh and heart. For example, the body will fail by sickness, age, and death, which touches the bone, and the flesh touches us deeply. When the flesh fails, the heart is ready to fall, too; the conduct, character, and courage can fail as well. However, it's when God is the strength of our hearts (inward man) that we find the strength to overcome.

"Therefore, we do not lose heart. Even though our outward man is perishing, yet the inward man is being renewed day by day. For our light affliction, which is but for a moment, is working for us a far more exceeding and eternal weight of glory, while we do not look at the things which are seen, but at the things which are not seen. For the things which are seen are temporary, but the things which are not seen are eternal." 2 Corinthians 4:16-18

Today, I pray that we never forget that HE IS the strength of our hearts and our portion forever (eternal).

DAY 150

Love One Another

"A new commandment I give to you, that you love one another; as I have loved you, that you also love one another. By this all will know that you are My disciples, if you have love for one another." John 13:34-35

It is evident in scripture that we are to love one another. But how do we love one another? God gives the Believer specific instructions:

"Beloved, if God so loved us, we also ought to love one another."
1 John 4:11

"And this commandment we have from Him: that he who loves God must love his brother also." 1 John 4:21

"For this is the message that you heard from the beginning, that we should love one another," 1 John 3:11

"If someone says, "I love God," and hates his brother, he is a liar; for he who does not love his brother whom he has seen, how can he love God whom he has not seen?" I John 4:20

"If someone says, "I love God," and hates his brother, he is a liar; for he who does not love his brother whom he has seen, how can he love God whom he has not seen? And this commandment we have from Him: that he who loves God must love his brother also." 1 John 4:20-21

254

Love is a distinct quality of a Believer. God is love, and He is conforming us into His image to be loving. Therefore, every Believer must prioritize love for God and love for others, especially for other Believers.

My prayer for you today is that you would experience HIS genuine love for you so that you can share that much-needed love with others.

DAY 151

Save Us

"Now therefore, O LORD our God, save us from his hand, that all the kingdoms of the earth may know that You are the LORD, You alone." Isaiah 37:20

This verse is part of the prayer that Hezekiah communicated, and then God responded by sending an angel of the Lord into the camp of the Assyrians. In one night's time, one hundred eighty-five thousand of the enemy were slaughtered by this invisible heavenly being. The few soldiers who remained went back to their homeland defeated. Miraculously the Israelites were spared without an arrow being shot or a spear being thrown. The Hebrew word *Yasha* is translated as "save"; it is also rendered "defend," "deliver," "rescue," and "preserve." He is "God our Savior" (1 Timothy 2:3), "the Savior of the world" (John 4:42), and "the Savior of all men" (1 Timothy 4:10). The very name Yeshua (Jesus) means "the salvation of God," and His name is a declaration of HIS nature. This salvation is who HE is. This salvation is what HE does. HE saves - and it's all for HIS glory!

My prayer for you today is that God would save you and that everyone who sees His blessings in your life will acknowledge Him as the source - giving Him the glory!

DAY 152

True Circumcision

"Beware of dogs, beware of evil workers, beware of the mutilation! For we are the circumcision, who worship God in the Spirit, rejoice in Christ Jesus, and have no confidence in the flesh," Philippians 3:2-3

Beware of dogs: This was a solid and harsh reference to the troublemaking legalists who attempted to deceive the Philippians. Interestingly, the term "Dogs" is exactly the term of contempt a Pharisee would use against Gentiles. Paul spoke volumes to those who found their righteousness from the law and not through faith in Christ. In other words, beware of men of a quarrelsome and contentious spirit, who under the false front of religion hide impure and unclean things; and who are not only defiled but defiling others in their influence.

Paul goes on to define three things that make for true circumcision:

1. Who worships God in the Spirit: They worship God in the Spirit instead of the fleshly and external worship emphasized by these legalists.
2. Rejoice in Christ Jesus: This also characterizes those of the true circumcision. Their joy is not found in their ability to be justified by the law or by their law-keeping. Jesus alone is their joy.
3. Have no confidence in the flesh: This is the third characteristic of the true circumcision. The follower of

Christ does not trust in their ability to be righteous before God through external works (the flesh), but their only confidence is in Jesus.

My prayer for us today is: "and be found in Him, not having my own righteousness, which is from the law, but that which is through faith in Christ, the righteousness which is from God by faith;" Philippians 3:9

DAY 153

Inspired By God

"All Scripture is given by inspiration of God, and is profitable for doctrine, for reproof, for correction, for instruction in righteousness, that the man of God may be complete, thoroughly equipped for every good work." 2 Timothy 3:16-17

Paul exhorted Timothy, "Continue in these things because the Bible comes from God and not man. It is a God-inspired book, breathed out from God Himself." This exhortation means something more than saying that God inspired the men who wrote it, though we believe that He did. God also inspired the very words they wrote. It's essential to notice that it doesn't say, "All Scripture writers are inspired by God," even though that was true. Yet, it doesn't go far enough. God breathed the words they wrote.

As you study about the Word of God, Repentance & Salvation, Water Baptism, Prayer & Fasting, Praise & Worship, The Holy Spirit, The Gifts of the Spirit, and Personal Evangelism, I pray that the scriptures would become personal and transforming in your life.

My prayer for us today is: "I beseech you therefore, brethren, by the mercies of God, that you present your bodies a living sacrifice, holy, acceptable to God, which is your reasonable service. And do not be conformed to this world, but be transformed by the renewing of your mind, that you may prove what is that good and acceptable and perfect will of God." Romans 12:1-2

DAY 154

He Is A Rewarder

"But without faith it is impossible to please Him, for he who comes to God must believe that He is, and that He is a rewarder of those who diligently seek Him." Hebrews 11:6

This statement is the foundation of faith that is required of any who seeks God. One must believe that He is, and one must believe He is a Rewarder of those who diligently seek Him. We must believe that God is there and that He will reveal Himself to the seeking heart.

The truth is, the very purpose of our existence is to bring pleasure to God. In the fourth chapter of the book of Revelation, John sees the cherubim about the throne of God, worshipping the Lord, declaring God's holiness and eternal character. The twenty-four elders fall on their faces before the throne and take their crowns and cast them on the glassy sea, and they say, "Thou art worthy, O Lord, to receive glory and honor; for You have created all things, and for Your pleasure they are and were created" (Revelation 4:11). A fundamental fact of our existence--you were created for God's pleasure. A person who lives for their pleasure is living out of sync with God. It is interesting to note how a person living for their pleasure continues to pursue more pleasures, constantly trying to find something new, something different, some new sensation, but are never satisfied. However, the rewards that come from seeking and worshiping God cannot be compared to any pleasure this world offers.

When we understand that HE is our reward, we seek no other glory but HIS. We find peace in knowing that HE is our everything.

My prayer for us today is that we would be able to say, "For I consider that the sufferings of this present time are not worthy to be compared with the glory which shall be revealed in us." Romans 8:18

DAY 155

In The Morning

"My voice You shall hear in the morning, O LORD; In the morning I will direct it to You, And I will look up." Psalm 5:3

It is believed that David made it a point to pray in the morning. He did this because he wanted to honor God at the beginning of his day and set the tone for an entire day dedicated to God. "But to You, I have cried out, O LORD, And in the morning my prayer comes before You." Psalm 88:13

The idea behind **"direct it to You"** is not "to aim" but "to order, to arrange." It is the word used for laying in order the wood and pieces upon the altar, and it is also used to put the shewbread upon the table. It means just this: 'I will arrange and order my prayer before the LORD;' I will lay it out upon the altar in the morning, just as the priest lays out the morning sacrifice.

There is something significant about giving God the first of every day. Its like laying a foundation on which to build a successful and fruitful day.

My prayer for us today is that we would declare His lovingkindness in the morning, And His faithfulness every night," Psalm 92:2

DAY 156

And I Will Heal Your Backsliding

"A voice was heard on the desolate heights, Weeping and supplications of the children of Israel. For they have perverted their way; They have forgotten the LORD their God. 'Return, you backsliding children, And I will heal your backsliding.' Indeed we do come to You, For You are the LORD our God." Jeremiah 3:21-22

My wife and I were recently praying for backsliders. We found ourselves broken for the pain and heartache they continue to have to navigate through. The truth is, the downward spiral of chaos and confusion are all attempts of the enemy of their soul to destroy their lives. However, what comes to mind is the Word of God. As long as there is breath, there is hope for the backslider to come home. They can experience peace, redemption, and restoration. The Word is our Hope:

"Restore to me the joy of Your salvation, And uphold me by Your generous Spirit." Psalm 51:12

"He restores my soul; He leads me in the paths of righteousness For His name's sake." Psalm 23:3

"Restore us, O LORD God of hosts; Cause Your face to shine, And we shall be saved!" Psalm 80:19

Please join us in praying for the backsliders to come home.

DAY 157

Filled with the Holy Spirit, and Prophesied

"Now his father Zacharias was filled with the Holy Spirit, and prophesied, saying." Luke 1:67

Prophesying is one of the byproducts of being "filled with the Spirit." We know this was a genuinely Spirit-inspired prophecy from Zachariah because the first focus is the unborn Jesus, not His newborn son John.

Zachariah is inspired to see the following (Read Luke 1:68-79):

* Jesus is **the horn of salvation for us** (v. 69)
* Jesus is the One who saves us from our enemies (v. 71)
* Jesus is the One **to perform the mercy promised to our fathers** (v. 72)
* Jesus is the One **to remember the covenant** (v. 72)
* Jesus makes us able to **serve Him without fear** (v. 74)
* Jesus gives **knowledge of salvation** to His people By the remission of their sins
* Jesus is the One to **give light** to those who sit in darkness and the shadow of death (v. 79)
* Jesus is the One to **guide our feet into the way of peace** (v. 79).

My conclusion is this, guard your heart against modern-day prophecy that does not focus on Jesus Christ. The same can be said about those who study the Book of Revelation. Remember, the Book is called a Revelation of Jesus Christ.

265

My prayer for us today is that we can discern what true prophecy is: "Then Jesus spoke to them again, saying, 'I am the light of the world. He who follows Me shall not walk in darkness, but have the light of life.'" John 8:12

DAY 158

A Different Spirit

"But My servant Caleb, because he has a different spirit in him and has followed Me fully, I will bring into the land where he went, and his descendants shall inherit it."
Numbers 14:24

God made it clear in Caleb's day that those who put God to the test and rebelled against His promise would not see the Promised Land. However, Caleb was known as a "servant" of God. His stand of faith and his "different spirit" would cause him to inherit the land.

I want Caleb's life to be an encouragement to us today. So may we be established and maintain a strong relationship with God daily, and despite the chaos all around us, let's keep a heart of a servant that is different from a society filled with hate and revenge.

A strong relationship with God produces assurance and boldness of faith to be different and to be able to believe for the impossible.

My prayer for us today is that we would be a people that can say with confidence, "I can do all things through Christ who strengthens me." Philippians 4:13

DAY 159

Live In Peace

"Finally, brethren, farewell. Become complete. Be of good comfort, be of one mind, live in peace; and the God of love and peace will be with you." 2 Corinthians 13:11

In the noisy and politically charged world we find ourselves in today, let us remember that the works of man rise and fall, but that true freedom is found in trusting "the God of love and peace." Only then will we truly understand what it means to "Be of good comfort, be of one mind, live in peace."

Friends, it is crucial to speak out for what we believe is correct and vote for the political candidates that we believe best reflect our deepest-held values. However, we must never forget that political systems rise and fall like all works of man. Remember, true freedom is found in trusting in Jesus Christ, listening patiently for His Word to us, and treating each other with the respect we all deserve as image-bearers of God. Then we will truly understand what it means to "live in peace."

There is a cost to work hard to be of good comfort, be of one mind, and live in peace, but the reward is worth it: the God of love and peace will be with you.

My prayer for you today is that you would "Become complete. Be of good comfort, be of one mind, live in peace, and the God of love and peace will be with you."

DAY 160

A More Excellent Way

"But earnestly desire the best gifts. And yet I show you a more excellent way." 1 Corinthians 12:31

Do you want to choose the more excellent way? Then build, strengthen, encourage, and bless others. This more excellent way is what love is all about.

"Love is patient and kind. Love is not jealous or boastful or proud, or rude. It does not demand its own way. It is not irritable, and it keeps no record of being wronged. It does not rejoice about injustice but rejoices whenever the truth wins out. Love never gives up, never loses faith, is always hopeful, and endures through every circumstance." 1 Corinthians 13:4-7 NLT

Will there be challenges? Yes! Will there be wrong actions by others? Yes! Will we be misunderstood? Yes! However, choose the way of love.

"Dear friends, let us continue to love one another, for love comes from God. Anyone who loves is a child of God and knows God." 1 John 4:7 NLT

I pray that we would walk in the "More Excellent Way" by looking for opportunities to share HIS love.

DAY 161

God's Love of Life Matters

"The thief does not come except to steal, and to kill, and to destroy. I have come that they may have life, and that they may have it more abundantly." John 10:10

Can you see from this verse how "Life" matters to God? How about the simple truth found in John 3:16? "For God so loved the world that He gave His only begotten Son, that whoever believes in Him should not perish but have everlasting life."

From scripture, we can also see that the opposite is true about the Devil and those in his control. Life does not matter to the enemy. In John 10:10, Thief implies deception and trickery; robber implies violence and destruction. These take away life, but Jesus gives life, and He gives it abundantly. These are the con men and muggers of what matters to God. These thieves and robbers who want to destroy are putting doubt and fear in people's lives who God sent His Son to redeem.

I find this simple truth working in me; the more I focus on who God is and what He has done, the less I worry or strive to make my life matter.

My prayer for us today is that we care more about what God says than what people say. "Jesus said to him, 'I am the way, the truth, and the life. No one comes to the Father except through Me.'" John 14:6

DAY 162

Riches

*"In Him we have redemption through His blood, the forgiveness of sins, according to the **riches** of His grace"*
Ephesians 1:7

Many seek "riches" for confidence, power, and peace. Unfortunately, people are being confused or deceived in what true riches are. Only when we search the scriptures will we find true meaning for life. "That in the ages to come He might show the exceeding riches of His grace in His kindness toward us in Christ Jesus." Ephesians 2:7

The redemption and forgiveness given are according to the measure of the riches of His grace. It is not a "small" redemption or forgiveness won by Jesus on the cross. It is HUGE!!!!!

We also read that God's riches are "unsearchable" and beyond what we can imagine or think. The Apostle Paul said it this way: "To me, who am less than the least of all the saints, this grace was given, that I should preach among the Gentiles the unsearchable riches of Christ," Ephesians 3:8

The truth be known, for the Believer, we will worship throughout eternity at the riches and measure of God's love and mercy.

My prayer for us today is: "And that He might make known the riches of His glory on the vessels of mercy, which He had prepared beforehand for glory," Romans 9:23

DAY 163

Abide In HIM

"Abide in Me, and I in you. As the branch cannot bear fruit of itself, unless it abides in the vine, neither can you, unless you abide in Me. 'I am the vine, you are the branches. He who abides in Me, and I in him, bears much fruit; for without Me you can do nothing.'" John 15:4-5

"Without Me, you can do nothing" It isn't that the disciples could do no activity without Jesus. They could be active without Him, as were the enemies of Jesus and many others. Yet, they could do nothing of real or eternal value without Jesus. Simply put, Jesus is the One who brings significance to us and makes our life worth living. Jesus also emphasized a mutual relationship. It isn't only that the disciple abides in the Master; the Master also abides in the disciple. This close relationship is described in Song of Solomon 6:3: I am my beloved's, and my beloved is mine. When Jesus says: Abide in me, He is talking about our will, our choices, and about the decisions we make. When we are abiding in Him, we are choosing to keep ourselves in contact with Him. This determination is what it means to "Abide in Me" (Jesus).

My prayer for us today is that we would "abide" in the One who will make our paths righteous.

DAY 164

Why Fast and Pray?

Jesus answered, 'Can you make the friends of the bridegroom fast while he is with them? But the time will come when the bridegroom will be taken away from them; in those days they will fast. '" Luke 5:34-35 (NIV)

We learn from this passage of scripture that there would come a day when fasting is appropriate for Jesus' followers. When Jesus was with the disciples, it was not the time to fast. However, we are now on that day that we must fast and pray. Therefore, I would like to give some reasons for fasting:

1. Fasting is all about endurance. The struggle between flesh and spirit would never be more robust than when we try to begin a fast and immediately after ending one.
2. Fasting will position our hearts to receive grace from the Lord, so a failure in fasting could rob us of the grace needed. Instead, when the Holy Spirit presses us too fast, we need to discover that He is preparing us for what is ahead.
3. Fasting is a spiritual exercise, and we become stronger with each attempt. However, more important than learning about the discipline of fasting, we gain knowledge of the object of our spiritual hunger. Jesus wants a deeper relationship with us.
4. Thousands of other Christians have walked this path before us. Many powerful, anointed servants of God paid the price by consistently participating in the discipline of fasting."

My prayer for us today is that we set times aside for prayer and fasting.

DAY 165

I Will Give You Rest

"Come to Me, all you who labor and are heavy laden, and I will give you rest. Take My yoke upon you and learn from Me, for I am gentle and lowly in heart, and you will find rest for your souls. For My yoke is easy and My burden is light." Matthew 11:28-30

Many people go to sleep at night, but they struggle to get rest. So I often ask my children in the morning if they slept well, and if they respond, "yes," I remind them to thank the LORD because rest is a gift from God.

Jesus described His gift to His followers as rest for your soul. This unmatchable gift is both powerful and profound. It is considered the birthright of those who come to Jesus and are His followers.

You will find rest for your souls is also an echo of the Hebrew text of Jeremiah 6:16, where it is the offer of God to those who follow his way; Jesus now issues the invitation in His own name.

Our nation is filled with unrest, and it won't get better for those who don't call upon the name of the Lord. Fires, floods, hurricanes, tornadoes, riots, racism, gangs, and disease. Our society is broken, and unfortunately, people are looking to the wrong priorities and the wrong solutions for rest.

I pray that you would experience rest for your soul and strength that comes from the ONE who upholds you with HIS righteous right hand. "Fear not, for I am with you; Be not dismayed, for I am your God. I will strengthen you, Yes, I will help you, I will uphold you with My righteous right hand." Isaiah 41:10

DAY 166

You Are Called

"I, therefore, the prisoner of the Lord, beseech you to walk worthy of the calling with which you were called,"
Ephesians 4:1

I believe everyone has a unique calling from the LORD. Unique in the sense that we do not all carry out the details of our calling the same. In other words, we all have some distinctive qualities. However, those who follow Jesus Christ have the following commissioning:

LIVING SACRIFICE
"I beseech you therefore, brethren, by the mercies of God, that you present your bodies a living sacrifice, holy, acceptable to God, which is your reasonable service." Romans 12:1

PROCLAIMING
"And He said to them, "Go into all the world and preach (proclaim) the gospel to every creature." Mark 16:15

TEACHING
"Go therefore and make disciples of all the nations, baptizing them in the name of the Father and of the Son and of the Holy Spirit, teaching them to observe all things that I have commanded you; and lo, I am with you always, even to the end of the age." Amen." Matthew 28:19-20

WARNING

"Him we preach, warning every man and teaching every man in all wisdom, that we may present every man perfect in Christ Jesus." Colossians 1:28

MINISTERING RECONCILIATION

"Therefore, if anyone is in Christ, he is a new creation; old things have passed away; behold, all things have become new. Now all things are of God, who has reconciled us to Himself through Jesus Christ and has given us the ministry of reconciliation," 2 Corinthians 5:17-18

My prayer for us today is that we would function in our unique callings but never neglect some of the distinctive qualities found in all followers of Christ.

DAY 167

A Savior Is Born

"Then the angel said to them, "Do not be afraid, for behold, I bring you good tidings of great joy which will be to all people. For there is born to you this day in the city of David a Savior, who is Christ the Lord. And this will be the sign to you: You will find a Babe wrapped in swaddling cloths, lying in a manger." And suddenly there was with the angel a multitude of the heavenly host praising God and saying: 'Glory to God in the highest, And on earth peace, goodwill toward men!'" Luke 2:10-14

It was an unforgettable night for the shepherds. A shining presence of an angel and the glory of the Lord appeared. Moreover, this first Angel brought good tidings (literally, it means that he preached the gospel) to these shepherds, who were regarded as social outcasts.

"For there is born to you this day in the city of David a Savior." The Angel announced the birth of the Savior. This announcement is what humanity needed on that day, and it is still needed today.

After the single Angel's announcement, a whole group of angels appeared. This appearance was a heavenly host (a band of soldiers) that proclaimed peace. The world needed the proclamation of this peace then, and it needs it now. Peace can only come when the gift of Jesus the Savior is received.

My prayer for us today is that we know and make known the gift of the Savior. "For the wages of sin is death, but the gift of God is eternal life in Christ Jesus our Lord." Romans 6:23

DAY 168

New Man

"This I say, therefore, and testify in the Lord, that you should no longer walk as the rest of the Gentiles walk, in the futility of their mind, having their understanding darkened, being alienated from the life of God, because of the ignorance that is in them, because of the blindness of their heart; who, being past feeling, have given themselves over to lewdness, to work all uncleanness with greediness. But you have not so learned Christ, if indeed you have heard Him and have been taught by Him, as the truth is in Jesus: that you put off, concerning your former conduct, the old man which grows corrupt according to the deceitful lusts, and be renewed in the spirit of your mind, and that you put on the new man which was created according to God, in true righteousness and holiness."
Ephesians 4:17-24

The Apostle Paul is reminding the church that there must be a break from the past. Jesus doesn't want to be added to our old life merely. Instead, the old life dies, and He becomes our new life. The ignorance and lack of understanding of man is a heart problem. This ignorance that we can live without God is a foolish denial and moral failure (licentiousness, uncleanness, greediness).

For the follower of Christ, our life must go beyond head knowledge. The knowledge of Christ is not just in the sense of knowing facts and information, but the ability to set our minds on the right things. This way of thinking is so fundamental for the Believer. Christ renews our minds.

My prayer for us today is: "And do not be conformed to this world, but be transformed by the renewing of your mind, that you may prove what is that good and acceptable and perfect will of God." Romans 12:2

DAY 169

Genuine Hope

"Rejoicing in hope, patient in tribulation, continuing steadfastly in prayer;" Romans 12:12

Paul says we serve God rejoicing in hope, not rejoicing in results. So the command is to do all these things with an eye towards heaven. It's also important to pray for HIS Kingdom to come and HIS will to be done on earth as it is in heaven.

Patient in tribulation does not indicate being passive or putting up with things, but active, steadfast, and filled with endurance. Tribulation expresses not some minor issue but deep and severe trouble or distress. We fulfill the command for hope, patience, and steadfast character described here through being patient in tribulation. The truth is, difficult times do not excuse us when we abandon hope or patience or continue steadfastly in prayer. Trials do not justify a lack of love in the body of Christ or a lack of willingness to do His work. The hope that tribulation builds in us is not a hope that will disappoint. "Now hope does not disappoint because the love of God has been poured out in our hearts by the Holy Spirit who was given to us" Romans 5:5. I believe our greatest hope usually has in mind our ultimate reward, which is Jesus.

My prayer for us today is that we have genuine hope: "This hope we have as an anchor of the soul, both sure and steadfast, and which enters the Presence behind the veil, where the forerunner has entered for us, even Jesus, having become High Priest forever according to the order of Melchizedek." Hebrews 6:19-20

DAY 170

Where Are You?

"Then the LORD God called to Adam and said to him, 'Where are you?'" Genesis 3:9

It's always interesting to hear of God asking someone a question that He already knows the answer to the question. It's evident to me that God has His way of causing us to search our hearts.

For many Jews and Christians throughout the world, in Fall, there is a celebration called the Feast of Trumpets, also known as Rosh Hashanah. Throughout the scriptures, we see God's heart to warn people before He executes His judgment. For example, God warned the people before the Flood and Nineveh before it was judged and destroyed. The feast of Trumpets reflects God's desire to summon His people to repentance so that He can vindicate them on the day is His judgment. The Feast of Trumpets fell on the first day of the seventh month, which stood out in the religious year as the Sabbatical month that ushered in the last three annual feasts, Trumpets, Atonement, and Tabernacles. These three feasts, known as "The High Holy Days," marked the conclusion of the religious year and ultimately the consummation of the plan of redemption.

For many religious Jews, the observance of the first day of the seventh month as Rosh Hashanah, the New Year of the civil and agricultural calendar, may have inspired the rabbinical tradition that Adam also was created on the same day. The Rabbis thought it was logical to assume that man should be judged on the Anniversary of His creation. This view influences the belief that humanity also would be judged on the same day. The Rabbis expressed confidence in God's mercy because just as God forgave Adam, so He would forgive those who repent during the Ten Days of Repentance. The Jews understood the shofar blowing on Rosh Hashanah as the beginning of their trial before the heavenly court, a test that lasted ten days until the Day of Atonement (Yom kipper). Just as God asked the question to Adam, "Where are you?", He still calls upon His people with the loud sounding of the shofar on Rosh Hashanah to repent and prepare to stand before His judgment seat. The Trumpets are sounding throughout the world, "Saying with a loud voice, 'Fear God and give glory to Him, for the hour of His judgment has come; and worship Him who made heaven and earth, the sea and springs of water.'" Revelation 14:7

The Jewish understanding of the Feast of Trumpets as an annual trumpet call to stand before God and seek His cleansing grace and mercy is most relevant for all believers in Christ today. Christians, too, need to be reminded that, "We must all appear before the judgment seat of Christ, so that each one may receive good and evil, according to what he has done in the body" (2 Corinthians 5:10). Thus, the Feast of Trumpets provides a much-needed annual wake-up call to prepare oneself to stand before God's judgment by repenting and forsaking sinful ways.

In conclusion, the Feast of Trumpets reflects God's desire to summon His people to repentance so that He can vindicate them on the day of His judgment. In other words, the question remains: "Where are you?"

My prayer for us today is that we humble ourselves before God and pray: "Create in me a clean heart, O God, And renew a steadfast spirit within me." Psalm 51:10

DAY 171

Save Sinners

"This is a faithful saying and worthy of all acceptance, that Christ Jesus came into the world to save sinners, of whom I am chief." 1 Timothy 1:15

There is a great danger in taking the terms sin and sinner out of our vocabulary. Many people are deliberately doing this today because they don't want to offend anyone. But if Jesus came to save sinners, shouldn't we announce it.

Since Jesus came into the world to save sinners, this is the first necessary qualification for being a child of God – recognizing your sin. After that, sinners are not disqualified from coming to God because Jesus came to save them.

Jesus came to save sinners, not those living under the illusion of their "own" righteousness. It is the sick who need a physician: "When Jesus heard it, He said to them, 'Those who are well have no need of a physician, but those who are sick. I did not come to call the righteous, but sinners, to repentance'" Mark 2:17. Jesus was and is the physician of the spirit, soul, and body.

My prayer for us today is that we never forget what God has rescued us from: "But God demonstrates His own love toward us, in that while we were still sinners, Christ died for us." Romans 5:8

DAY 172

Confession & Belief

"For God so loved the world that He gave His only begotten Son, that whoever believes in Him should not perish but have everlasting life. For God did not send His Son into the world to condemn the world, but that the world through Him might be saved. He who believes in Him is not condemned, but he who does not believe is condemned already because he has not believed in the name of the only begotten Son of God." John 3:16-18

John 3:16 is the most generous and fantastic offer conceivable – eternal life for all who believe. Yet the offer has inherent consequences for any who reject, who refuse to believe. Their refusal makes their condemnation sure. In other words, this was a combined promise of salvation and a warning.

It is apparent in the scriptures that we do not gain God's righteousness by works. Instead, we achieve it by confessing and believing in the person and work of Jesus Christ. So salvation rests on confession and belief. "That if you confess with your mouth the Lord Jesus and believe in your heart that God has raised Him from the dead, you will be saved. For with the heart one believes unto righteousness, and with the mouth, confession is made unto salvation. For the Scripture says, 'Whoever believes on Him will not be put to shame.'" Romans 10:9-11

"This is the condemnation": Jesus came to bring salvation, but those who reject that salvation condemn themselves.

My prayer for us today is that we do what Jesus said: "And He said to them, "Go into all the world and preach the gospel to every creature. He who believes and is baptized will be saved; but he who does not believe will be condemned." Mark 16:15-16

DAY 173

Delivered From All My Fears

"I sought the LORD, and He heard me, And delivered me from all my fears." Psalm 34:4

What does it mean to be delivered? This Psalm has the idea of being snatched away, rescued, saved, or plundered away from all fear. God knows we all need this deliverance today.

We also learn from this verse that David's prayers ("sought" means seeking the LORD in prayer) helped silence his fears. Thus, having sought the Lord, David, the Psalmist, surrendered his situations and circumstances to the LORD.

Here is the way I read this verse: "I sought the Lord, in my distress, entreated His favor, begged His help, and He heard me, answered my request immediately, and delivered me from all my fears, both from the death I feared and from the worry and anxiousness produced by the fear of it.

My prayer for us today is that we experience the delivering power of the LORD. "Save us and help us with your right hand, that those you love may be delivered." Psalm 60:5 NIV

DAY 174

Let My People Go

"....Let My people go, that they may hold a feast to Me in the wilderness." Exodus 5:1

The underlying demand of God to Pharaoh (through His messengers Moses and Aaron) was freedom for His people. God made it clear that Israel belonged to Him, not Pharaoh, and therefore, the people of God should be free. Those who belong to God should be free, not bound. At least seven times (Exodus 5:1; 7:16; 8:1; 8:20; 9:1; 9:13; 10:3), the LORD has Moses go before Pharaoh to declare, "Let My people go, that they may serve Me." Here are some basic conclusions from the repetition of this request:

1. God is serious about us serving (worshiping) HIM.
2. Even though God speaks to you, it isn't always well received.
3. Obedience doesn't always bring about immediate blessings.

I am convinced that the closer we walk with the LORD, the greater our burden will become to see people set free to serve the LORD.

My prayer for us today is that we would be free to worship: "But the hour is coming, and now is, when the true worshipers will worship the Father in spirit and truth; for the Father is seeking such to worship Him." John 4:23

DAY 175

The Power of Words

"Death and life are in the power of the tongue, And those who love it will eat its fruit." Proverbs 18:21

Your words can diminish your life, or they can add purpose to your journey. They can curse your destiny, or they can bless your future. What you're saying in the storm will determine how long you will stay in that storm. Most importantly, don't talk about how big your problems are. Instead, talk about how faithful your God is.

Under the terms of the Old Covenant, Israel had a choice: life or death, good or evil. It was up to them. God was going to glorify Himself through Israel one way or another. How it would happen was their choice. "See, I have set before you today life and good, death and evil, in that, I command you today to love the LORD your God, to walk in His ways, and to keep His commandments, His statutes, and His judgments, that you may live and multiply; and the LORD, your God, will bless you in the land which you go to possess." Deuteronomy 30:15-16

Those who are wise enough to love and appreciate the power of what they say will be blessed by the fruit of their speech.

My prayer for us today is: "Let your speech always be with grace, seasoned with salt, that you may know how you ought to answer each one." Colossians 4:6

DAY 176

Your Labor In Not In Vain

"But thanks be to God, who gives us the victory through our Lord Jesus Christ. Therefore, my beloved brethren, be steadfast, immovable, always abounding in the work of the Lord, knowing that your labor is not in vain in the Lord."

If we are honest, we've all lost some battles in our life. And at times, we have all struggled to see what good can come out of our present struggle. However, when we take our focus off ourselves and onto the victory of our LORD and SAVIOR, we find peace and rest. It is the victory of Jesus Christ that ultimately brings about our success. It is His victory that makes us steadfast, immovable, always abounding in the work of the Lord! We don't need to waver, we don't need to doubt or fear, we don't need to fall, and we don't need to quit! The Lord will show His remembrance of our work and labor of love at the resurrection. As the Hebrew writer acknowledges: "For God is not unjust to forget your work and labor of love which you have shown toward His name, in that you have ministered to the saints, and do minister" (Hebrews 6:10).

Even if your work is vain to everyone else, and everyone else discounts or doesn't appreciate what you do for the Lord, your labor is not in vain in the Lord. It doesn't matter if you get the praise or the encouragement. The truth is, sometimes you will, and sometimes you won't. The main thing is that we live to please the LORD.

My prayer for you today is that you would "be steadfast, immovable, always abounding in the work of the Lord, knowing that your labor is not in vain in the Lord."

DAY 177

Value

"Death and life are in the power of the tongue, And those who love it will eat its fruit." Proverbs 18:21

Two questions come to mind today?

#1 Where does value come from in your life? - PAUSE

#2 Do I value my words? In other words, do I place a value on what I am speaking? - PAUSE

God wants us to learn to value what He values. This admonition is why we are instructed: "So then, my beloved brethren, let every man be swift to hear, slow to speak, slow to wrath" (James 1:19). The Psalmist David also reminds us of this vital instruction when he prays, "Let the words of my mouth and the meditation of my heart be acceptable in Your sight, O LORD, my strength and my Redeemer" (Psalm 19:14).

Again, those who are wise enough to love and appreciate the power of what they say will be blessed and will eat the pleasant fruit of wise and valued speech.

My prayer for us today is that we value our words, knowing they are powerful. "In the multitude of words, sin is not lacking, but he who restrains his lips is wise." Proverbs 10:19

DAY 178

Boasting

"For by grace you have been saved through faith, and that not of yourselves; it is the gift of God, not of works, lest anyone should boast." Ephesians 2:8-9

God did it "not of works" simply so that no one could boast. If salvation was the accomplishment of man in any way, we could boast about it. But under God's plan of salvation, God alone receives the glory. The fact that boasting is mentioned in the scriptures tells me that it can be a problem. This problem stems from pride which is a direct influence by satan. Satan, from the beginning, has worked at discrediting and diminishing God's eternal plan through Jesus Christ.

It is apparent in the scriptures that we do not receive God's righteousness by works. Instead, we gain it by confessing and believing in the person and work of Jesus Christ. For example: "that if you confess with your mouth the Lord Jesus and believe in your heart that God has raised Him from the dead, you will be saved. For with the heart one believes unto righteousness, and with the mouth, confession is made unto salvation. For the Scripture says, 'Whoever believes on Him will not be put to shame.'" Romans 10:9-11

My prayer is that we learn from the words of the Apostle Paul when he said, "...yet of myself I will not boast, except in my infirmities. For though I might desire to boast, I will not be a fool; for I will speak the truth. But I refrain, lest anyone should think of me above what he sees me to be or hears from me." 2 Corinthians 12:5-6

DAY 179

Sins Have Hidden His Face

"Behold, the LORD's hand is not shortened, That it cannot save; Nor His ear heavy, That it cannot hear. But your iniquities have separated you from your God; And your sins have hidden His face from you, So that He will not hear. For your hands are defiled with blood, And your fingers with iniquity; Your lips have spoken lies, Your tongue has muttered perversity. No one calls for justice, Nor does any plead for truth. They trust in empty words and speak lies; They conceive evil and bring forth iniquity." Isaiah 59:1-4

In Isaiah the Prophets day, the people wondered why God did not seem to rescue them from their trials. They wondered if perhaps God had diminished in strength or if His hand had become shortened.

The Prophet clarifies that the problem isn't with God's power, His knowledge, or His interest. The problem is with their iniquities. Sin has separated them from their God.

Sin, however, does not separate us from the love of God because God loves sinners (Romans 5:8). However, sin does separate.
- Sin separates us from fellowship with God.
- Sin separates us from the blessing of God.
- Sin separates us from some of the benefits of God's love, even as the Prodigal Son, Luke 15:11-32, was still loved by the father but didn't enjoy the benefits of his love when he was in sin.

300

The answer to our separation is obvious: "Therefore say to the house of Israel, 'Thus says the Lord GOD: Repent, turn away from your idols, and turn your faces away from all your abominations.'" Ezekiel 14:6

"Repent therefore and be converted, that your sins may be blotted out, so that times of refreshing may come from the presence of the Lord," Acts 3:19

"Remember therefore from where you have fallen; repent and do the first works, or else I will come to you quickly and remove your lampstand from its place—unless you repent." Revelation 2:5

"As many as I love, I rebuke and chasten. Therefore be zealous and repent." Revelation 3:19

"For if you return to the LORD, your brethren and your children will be treated with compassion by those who lead them captive, so that they may come back to this land; for the LORD your God is gracious and merciful, and will not turn His face from you if you return to Him." 2 Chronicles 30:9

My prayer for us today is that we rejoice in this hope: "If we confess our sins, He is faithful and just to forgive us our sins and to cleanse us from all unrighteousness." 1 John 1:9

DAY 180

Be Strong & Very Courageous

"Only be strong and very courageous, that you may observe to do according to all the law which Moses My servant commanded you; do not turn from it to the right hand or to the left, that you may prosper wherever you go." Joshua 1:7

Courage is the steadfastness of faith. Courage looks up to the Lord and counts upon Him to give the victory in the conflict. For the LORD your God is with you wherever you go: The final encouragement, repeated from Joshua 1:5 & 9, reminds us that Joshua's success did not depend solely on his ability to keep God's Word. It, however, relied even more on God's presence with him. This steadfast faith in the LORD is ultimately where our courage comes from in our lives.

Courage and strength are not matters of feeling and circumstance. They are matters of choice, especially when God makes His strength available to us. We can be strong in the Lord and in the power of His might (Ephesians 6:10).

I've heard it said: It doesn't take courage to hate, but instead, it takes courage to love when you are surrounded by hate.

God uses courageous individuals to be encouraging people to help us fulfill the destiny He has for us.

My prayer for us today is that we would be strong and very courageous. "Wait on the LORD; Be of good courage, And He shall strengthen your heart; Wait, I say, on the LORD!

AUTHOR

Dr. Alan James Schrader has been in ministry for over 30 years, ordained through the International Fellowship of Christian Assemblies (IFCA). Alan and his wife Mary have pioneered Churches, ministered in many countries around the world, and started IFCA Bible College & Seminary and IFCA Bible Institute. Both Mary and Alan have a passion for effectively impacting lives by making fruitful Disciples of Christ. Alan also serves as Chaplain at Concord Reserve (Senior living community) in Westlake, Ohio, and a volunteer Chaplain for the Police Department in Richmond Heights, Ohio.

Contact:
Alan James Schrader
25595 Chardon Road
Cleveland, OH 44143
Email: Drajschrader@gmail.com.
Website: www.AlanJamesSchrader.com

The 30 Day Devotional & Journal (Daily Walking and Talking With Your Creator)

Winter DEVOTIONS (Part of the Daily Devotion Series)

Spring DEVOTIONS (Part of the Daily Devotion Series)

Summer DEVOTIONS (Part of the Daily Devotion Series)

Fall DEVOTIONS (Part of the Daily Devotion Series)

BASICS - *Christianity 101*

Introduction to Theology

Biblical Christianity vs. Other Religions

Financial   Freedom (Teachers Manual)

An Introduction to the Old Testament Scriptures (Teachers Manual)

Made in the USA
Middletown, DE
21 November 2021